$4.00

Women's Studies

by Gail Thomas McLure
John W. McLure

National Education Association
Washington, D.C.

Oakton Community College
Morton Grove, Illinois

WOMEN'S STUDIES

Copyright © 1977
National Education Association of the United States

Stock No. 1821-4-00 (paper)
1822-2-00 (cloth)

Note:

The opinions expressed in this publication should not be construed as representing the policy or position of the National Education Association. Materials published as part of the NEA *Developments in Classroom Instruction Series* are intended to be discussion documents for teachers who are concerned with specialized interests of the profession.

Library of Congress Cataloging in Publication Data

McLure, Gail Thomas.
  Women's studies.

  (Developments in classroom instruction)
  Bibliography: p.
  1. Women's studies. 2. Sex role.
I. McLure, John W., joint author. II. Title.
III. Series.
HQ1180.M23   301.41′2′071   77-22696
ISBN 0-8106-1822-2
ISBN 0-8106-1821-4 pbk.

CONTENTS

1.   Introduction: Women's Studies K-12

This book is focused on the curriculum changes needed to eliminate sex role stereotypes and on a new model for achieving psychological androgyny by means of women's studies. The achievement of psychological androgyny—a climate in which men and women will be able to develop freely without the inhibitions and constraints of sex roles—is our underlying concern.

As efforts to eliminate sex role stereotyping in the schools have gained momentum over the past few years, the meanings attached to the term "women's studies" have increased. Therefore this book is designed to help educators decide what women's studies should consist of in their school systems.

Women's studies are not limited to a study of the history of women. Nor are they made up of content strictly for women. Women's studies not only may but should be taught for boys as well as girls, by men as well as women.

Women's studies are not a fad any more than predominantly male history or vocational training for boys has been a fad. Changing roles of men and women should be taught because they are a fact of modern life that has an impact on the way in which today's students define their world. We cannot dictate today the relationship between the sexes tomorrow; but we can equip students to think about the kind of relationships they would like and the degree of androgyny nearest to the ideals of democracy. We can help them analyze the tradition that has kept women in low-paying, low-status jobs, that has prevented all but the most talented women from developing self-confidence and self-esteem, and that has contributed to women's feelings of powerlessness and self-sacrificing passivity. We can portray a more realistic view of women's potential and of their past contributions.

Every boy and girl should see reality in school activities. Reality about women's lives in history has been missing. Men's and women's lives are changing in basic ways, and the changing reality

7

should be reflected in school-related activities. Girls should experience parent and teacher expectations for their futures in as great diversity as boys. They should develop interests to match their individual aptitudes instead of their gender—interests that extend to mathematics, science, political science, mechanics, medicine, engineering, and law. Girls should experience positive rewards and reinforcement from their peers and significant adults for their participation in activities atypical of women. They should learn to be assertive, to be comfortable with the prospect of sharing household chores and child rearing, and to see multiple life-styles from which to choose.

Boys should learn about nurturance, family living, and nutrition; and they should learn to feel comfortable with the expression of a wider range of emotions. Boys should learn to view women and girls in a positive light, seeing females as individuals who have a diversity of interests, abilities, and values, and who share equal rights and expectations in career planning. Boys should have freedom from sanctions against their participation in activities previously considered atypical for their sex, and they should learn to acknowledge and appreciate intelligence in girls. Males should be encouraged to derive some of their sense of personal identity from healthy human relationships, from hobbies, and from domestic skills as well as from career orientations.

We can facilitate the growth of both sexes toward greater development of their own unique capabilities rather than toward those traits previously viewed as acceptable only for one sex or the other. Conformity to sex role standards has limited both sexes in their repertoire of appropriate behaviors and responses and limited self-expression to stereotyped patterns. Women's studies should encourage boys and girls to acquire character traits and to respond to situations in ways that promote effective results and contribute to self-esteem.

Women's studies cannot be adequately taught without recognizing that women often face not only sex discrimination but also oppression or exclusion of some other type as well. A critical feature of women's studies is the overlap with studies of racial, ethnic, and minority groups, including the handicapped and the oppressed. Cultural patterns affect women differently from one group to another, yet each contains many useful and powerful analogies for women. Gunnar Myrdal recognized this fact years ago in his classic work, *An American Dilemma*, on the Black American experience.[1]

As students become aware of the general ways in which their own lives are affected by sex role stereotypes, they will be better equipped to understand the subtle ways in which sex roles differ among various cultural groups. These different cultural groups may begin their pursuit of psychological androgyny from different points, move at different speeds, use different methods, and achieve varying results; but the promise of fuller, richer, and freer lives is the same.

What Are Women's Studies K-12?

It is easier to define women's studies on the college level than women's studies K-12. At the college level women's studies are courses, or programs of study, about the history, sociology, economics, and welfare of women, usually in the context of strategies for improving the status of women and for eliminating sex role stereotypes. At the secondary level such units and courses also exist, and there are related lessons at the elementary level.

But though this type of curriculum forms a very significant part of women's studies K-12, it does not form the whole. Grade school and secondary students participate in a far more varied instructional process than college students. Students K-12 learn not just from lessons specifically designed to teach students about the roles and contributions of women. They also learn about the status of women and girls from the attitudes of their teachers, from course requirements, from staffing patterns in the schools, from special recognitions and encouragements, and from the differential treatment of males and females in all school activities and materials.

Students learn from direct teaching about the changing roles of both sexes and sex role stereotyping, and such direct teaching should be a part of every teacher's lesson plans and every counselor's group guidance sessions. But direct teaching will not suffice if indirect messages about the role and status of women belie these messages.

Unless women are portrayed in elementary science books as making valuable contributions to that field, a course in high school which calls attention to such contributions may have little impact in encouraging girls to consider careers in science. If social studies teachers acknowledge the role of women in society only in a women's studies course, they may inadvertently accord women the status of a special interest group requiring a modicum of attention in a discipline which otherwise deals with more important matters. The content of women's studies may fall upon unreceptive ears if it is presented only in a special course or unit somewhere prior to graduation.

Women's studies, then, should appear as direct teaching and counseling; but perhaps even more importantly, they should also appear as indirect learning. Women's studies are both curricular and extracurricular studies and activities, and they must be comprehensive because all aspects of the school experience are affected. Women's studies K-12 should be carefully integrated into all segments of the curriculum, into teacher behavior, into guidance procedures, and into administrative policy. Women's studies K-12 should be so well integrated into instructional procedures and school policies that students will seldom be able to recognize that a special effort had to be made to acknowledge the other half of the human race.

Women's studies may include:

1. A discussion in an eighth grade industrial class about careers in science, engineering and technology.

2. A body-building program with equal encouragement for girls.

3. An exercise for fourth graders in counting the numbers and types of activities in which each sex participates in a given chapter of a mathematics or spelling book.

4. A reading lesson in a junior high language arts class about the effects of sexist language.

5. A driver education class which discusses the effects of sexist jokes on male and female drivers.

6. A vocational education teacher's encouraging remarks to a girl who is interested in auto mechanics.

7. A library display of books about women in mathematics.

8. An assembly program about the Women's International Year.

9. A bulletin board about the changing roles of men and women.

10. A lesson in a psychology class about men and women and attitudes toward success.

Today a transition period exists in many schools. Women's studies are offered as separate units, special-interest-day topics, and full-fledged courses. These forms reflect the shapes of college courses, but their separateness and their emphasis on women may be the cause of the cries of "reverse sexism" as Black studies were once accused of being the cause of "counter racism."

A major long-term goal of women's studies as a separate topic may be to create its own obsolescence. If the history and sociology of women were adequately reflected in the social studies curriculum, if textbooks and materials in all classes did not reflect a stereotyped image of each sex, if courses of study and extracurricular activities did not harbor underlying as well as overt assumptions about the role of women as distinct from the role of men, then women's studies as a separate topic might not be so urgent. When revised curriculum materials and processes are integrated into science, mathematics, industrial education, American history, and other parts of the course of study, keeping women's studies organized into large, aggregate units will no longer be necessary.

If women did not face a job market where they are often hired in token representation and later ignored by "old boy" higher-ups, if every other newsstand and many commercials on television did not proclaim women to be weak and confused objects for exploitation, then women's studies could disappear into the woodwork of the curriculum.

But this integration is not likely to occur for some time. After all, the problem of stereotyped sex roles touches upon all of our lives, male and female. Changes in these roles affect the cognitive structures around which we have organized most of what we know about humanity since earliest childhood. Even if we as educators could reorganize our own psyches and our classrooms to present women's studies in the best way imaginable, we would still be working with students who have been exposed to sex stereotyped assumptions since birth, who have grown up with sexist television programming and commercials, who use libraries full of biased books and materials, and who have heard parents say "Boys will be boys" and "Nice girls don't do that."

The task before us is immense.

2. Need for Changes in Sex Roles

Sex roles as rigid cultural institutions appear to have outlived their usefulness. The concept of sex roles has been defined as the institutionalization of those behaviors, values, attitudes, and expectations which a society regards as appropriate for one sex or the other. Sex roles mean a division of labor that presumes basic functions are assigned to, and managed by, people socialized and trained to perform them. As times have changed, people no longer live so close to the margin of physical survival, and the division of labor associated with child bearing, nursing, and rearing has become less a cultural accommodation to a biological reality and more a violation of other aspects of human biology and culture.

In their cultural analysis of sex roles and the school in a recent issue of the *Journal of Teacher Education*, Lee and Gropper ask us to consider the many men and women who, for reasons of temperament or training, are unsuited to their designated sex roles and assume them with great difficulty or fail to assume them at all, thus creating stress for themselves and society.[1] Stress is also created when society awards a higher status to one sex than to the other. Sex roles threaten the full development of human resources because people are restricted by cultural prescriptions rather than by individual aptitude or merit. Lee and Gropper also point out that traditional notions of sex role have been challenged by changes in contemporary life.[2]

12

Changes in Technology

New appliances, detailed directions, and recipes have made it possible for men and women to share homemaking roles. Industry has developed machines and processes which no longer require large outlays of physical strength and uncommon agility. For example, during World War II the shipbuilding companies dramatically altered their assembly lines for the convenience of the women workers, the "Rosie the Riveters."

Technology has enormously affected health. Advances in contraception, sterilization, and abortion have had an impact upon birth rates and upon attitudes toward sexuality as a recreational pursuit as well as a procreational necessity. Women have been able to take more effective control of their own bodies as a result. New diagnostic techniques and treatments in nutrition and medicine have reduced the terrors of childbearing, brought renewed hope to victims of disease, and helped to increase the life expectancy of both sexes. The percentage of Americans over age 65 has increased, and most of these older Americans are women.

Changes in the Cultural Institutions of Marriage and Family

Alternative forms of marriage and family have appeared in American society. In *The Future of Marriage* Jessie Bernard outlines several life-styles including privatized homes, cooperative households, communal neighborhoods or communities, and communal households.[3]

Concurrent developments include experimental and contractual arrangements of living together and an accelerating divorce rate. Lee and Gropper note three effects from increases in divorce: first, our view that marriage is a lifelong arrangement is undergoing revision; second, remarriage and shifts in family membership are seen as a normal occurrence; and third, the single-parent family has become a more significant phenomenon.

Women and World of Work

The present era of feminism is not the first time that women have appeared in industry outside the home. The Revolutionary War, the Civil War, and World War's I and II brought critical demands for labor, and many women entered unaccustomed occupations. Indeed, the percentages of women in a number of traditional fields such as education, have declined since the 1920's.

Statistics from the Women's Bureau of the U. S. Department of Labor show that more than 40 percent of women work. Men are no longer the sole breadwinners for their families—if such was ever the case. Women are both raising families and working in a variety of arrangements. Some stay home during child rearing years while others continue their outside jobs. A few couples are experimenting with sharing one job equally.

These changing work patterns have many implications for child nurturing and for relations between the sexes. The continued health and vigor of older Americans ia also quite possibly affected; and it is the hypothesis of some physicians that because older American men have been sex stereotyped they dissociate themselves from day-to-day activities following retirement. These men demonstrate a smaller range of activity because, for example, they see no reason to do the grocery shopping or to purchase a present for a grandchild as readily as their wives do. If greater sharing of roles does occur in the future, older men may stay active and healthy and live to a greater age than heretofore.

Laws

Familiar to most of us by now is the basic statement of Title IX of the Education Amendments of 1972 which reads:

> No person shall, on the basis of sex, be excluded from participation, be denied the benefits of, or be subjected to discrimination under any education program or activity receiving federal financial assistance.[4]

Less familiar, yet more directly relevant is the Regulation to implement Title IX, the first phase of which became effective July 21, 1975.[5] This Regulation outlines criteria for achieving compliance with Title IX.

The Women's Educational Equity Act of 1974, which had its rules and regulations published in 1976, authorized a three-year federal program of federal grants and contracts to further educational equity for women.[6] Even those educational agencies not receiving grants or contracts through this effort will stand to benefit because of this program's emphasis on national capacity building.

Community groups in many states have worked to call attention

14

to the need for women's studies in schools. For example, in 1971 a coalition of 42 women's rights groups in Pennsylvania was successful in getting their state's Department of Education to establish a task force to develop policies and programs that would eliminate systematic sex discrimination in schools. John C. Pittinger, the state's Commissioner of Education, issued a memorandum shortly after he took office in 1971 urging educators to seek ways to encourage equal opportunity for women and members of racial minorities in educational agencies with which his office had contracts.[7] This pressure was intended to reach to the local districts. Today school officials are feeling that pressure. Similar actions by feminists in other states have affected both legal and extralegal change.

Decade for Women: 1976–85

The United Nations proclaimed 1975 International Women's Year. The objective of the Year was to launch a cooperative effort among women of the world to define a world or society in which women could participate fully in economic, social, and political life, and to devise plans for achieving such a goal. A ten-year World Plan of Action grew out of the July 1975 meeting in Mexico City. The United Nations has proclaimed 1976–85 the Decade for Women and during this time the objectives of the International Women's Year will serve as guidelines for action. The World Plan of Action has outlined minimum goals for the first five years (1975–80) that include: increased civic education for women; coeducational technical and vocational training; equal access to education at every level; increased employment opportunities for women; reduction of unemployment and greater efforts to eliminate discrimination in employment; greater participation of women in policymaking positions at all levels; increased provision for health education, nutrition, family education, and family planning; recognition of the economic value of women's work in the home, in food production and marketing, and in voluntary activities; and direction of formal, informal, and lifelong education toward the re-evaluation of men and women in order to insure their full realization as individuals in the family and in society.[8]

Educational goals outlined in the World Plan of Action for the Decade for Women incorporate major goals of the women's movement that emerged in this country during the first half of the 1970's.

For example, the World Plan calls for new textbooks and school materials to reflect new attitudes toward roles of men and women in society and to reflect an image of women in positive and participatory roles in society. Vocational and career guidance programs should encourage both boys and girls to select careers according to their real aptitudes rather than according to sex role stereotypes. Scholarships and study grants should be equally available to both sexes. Women wishing to return to work after stepping out to raise a family should find help readily available. Research to identify discriminatory practices in education and new teaching techniques to correct them are urged. Women's studies represent organized efforts of educators to encourage such research and to incorporate new teaching techniques as well as new content into the classroom.

3. Women's Studies on the College Campus

For the past decade the term "women's studies" has meant a course, sometimes a program of courses, usually on a college campus. The term has come into common usage because of obvious discrepancies between the current content of education and that needed to acknowledge fully the dignity and human worth of women. According to Howe and Ahlum, the central ideas of women's studies are sex bias and the status of women.[1] Courses in women's studies have examined women's history, their contemporary condition, and their prescribed sex roles, frequently in the context of strategies for change in the lives of both sexes and in societal institutions. Women's studies courses are built on the premise that women have been both stereotyped and ignored by mediators of the culture. On college campuses such courses have supplied new knowledge about women, their contributions, their unrealized potential, and their new visions of and preferences for the future. The rapid growth of women's studies on college campuses is reflected in the fact that between the years 1971 and 1973 the number of courses increased from 600 to over 2,000.[2] By 1975 more than 5,000 courses on women's studies had been identified.[3]

Women's Studies in Schools of Education

According to a 1974 survey of 1,200 institutions of teacher education by the Resource Center on Sex Roles in Education, at least 184 women's studies courses have been or are being offered in teacher preparation programs.[4] This number represents rapid growth since 1970 when The Clearinghouse on Women's Studies could identify only four such courses in teacher preparation programs.

Four primary emphases characterizing women's studies courses offered in schools or colleges of education are described and critiqued by McCune and Matthews as follows:

1. General awareness or consciousness raising

2. Understanding the socialization process

3. Understanding historical, legal, and professional issues

4. Examining or modifying instructional practices.[5]

Although the four courses provided valuable beginnings, the reviewers note several limitations. Male sex role socialization and stereotyping has been inadequately considered. Behavioral science research and knowledge have been inadequately translated into implications for educational theory, practices, and reform. Significant trends or developments in educational theory or practice (e.g., individualized instruction) have seldom been applied to the elimination of sex role stereotyping or discrimination. The development and application of relevant educational skills have been unduly subordinated to the promotion of personal growth of students in the courses. Desired objectives and outcomes for schools, classrooms, and pupils have not been adequately addressed. Cultural, racial, ethnic, and socio-economic differences related to sex role stereotyping need to be more fully covered. Courses have suffered because professional literature in the field of education often does not reflect existing knowledge of sex role stereotyping and discrimination. The elective nature of the courses and the lack of integration of the relevant content throughout the education curriculum mean that only limited numbers of educators benefit.

As a part of their review of women's studies in colleges of education, McCune and Matthews make several recommendations for teacher educators. First, all faculty members should be involved in delineating and applying sex role issue content relevant to education and should participate in the development of plans to insure that such information is included in the prescribed curriculum. Second, students should learn about the implications of sex role socialization for schools. They should learn to develop nonsexist curriculum, to engage in nonsexist classroom interaction and management, and to participate in nonsexist administrative practices. Students should learn to work effectively with the community and with other professional educators to accomplish necessary change. Third, an adequate number of courses should be developed in the colleges of education to accomplish these goals for students. Fourth, faculty members should update their own knowledge and skills. Fifth, faculty should encourage in-service and continuing education among educators in the field.

4. Definitions, Concepts, and Theories

Definitions of sexism, sex role socialization, and sex role stereotypes have been standardized recently in regulations governing the award of federal funds appropriated for the Women's Educational Equity Act of 1974.[1] Sexism, according to those regulations, means the collection of attitudes, beliefs, and behaviors that reflect stereotyping or differentiation between the sexes on any basis other than physiological differences. In the context of schools, the term refers to those policies, practices, and activities that overtly or covertly structure both the development of girls and boys as well as the patterns of governance and employment. Sex role socialization, according to the same regulations, refers to the differential processes and experiences used to prepare males and females for the roles that society defines as being appropriate for their sex. Sex role stereotypes derive from assumptions that because females and males share a common gender, they also share common abilities, interests, values, and roles. The socialization process by which children and adults are prepared to occupy various roles is described by the same regulation as an accumulation of life experiences that transmits the knowledge, attitudes, and skills to perform functions necessary for these roles. The socialization of young children as they are being prepared to carry out a complex collection of economic, social, physical, political, and psychological roles as adults is often deliberate and readily observable. Much of adult socialization is subtle and unnoticed because it consists of continued reinforcement for already learned roles, even though it may become extremely focused and explicit in situations where the learning of new roles or skills is necessary.

The shift in the values of our society is clearly illustrated in the rise to popular understanding of these terms and their definitions. A few years ago educators promoted the concept of sex role development because they placed a high value on acquiring the patterns of behavior, skills, or attitudes defined by our culture as sex appropriate. Now many of the same educators are acknowledging the serious limitations placed on each sex by these cultivated sex roles.

Behaviors, skills, or attitudes equally appropriate to both sexes are, by definition, not related to sex roles; but those associated with one sex more than the other are referred to as *sex-typed*. The unwritten rules determining which behaviors, skills, and attitudes are sex-typed and which are not have been called *sex role standards*.[2] The term "masculinity" refers to the culturally defined sex role standard for males, and "femininity" refers to the culturally defined sex role standard for females.

Sex role standards are culturally determined notions that extend beyond the biological distinctions between males and females. Many of us are aware of the efforts of Maccoby and others who evaluated hundreds of studies of sex differences in order to determine which of these differences are real and which are mythical.[3] Unlike physical differences, most of the psychological differences between the two sexes seem to be tied to the culturally defined sex role standards of masculinity and femininity.

One exception seems to be the tendency of boys to be more aggressive than girls, both physically and verbally, though both sexes become less aggressive as they mature. Differences between sexes in verbal ability, mathematical reasoning, and spatial ability also appear at various times; but they are not consistent at all age levels. Waber has recently reported evidence that the difference in mental abilities may be more related to later maturation than to sex.[4] She found that early maturers—whether male or female—scored better on verbal than spatial tasks, but late maturers scored in the opposite direction. Since boys mature later on the average than girls, differences in mental abilities result in higher norms for boys on spatial and visual problems and higher norms for girls on verbal tasks.

In a 1942 report on data on sex differences in school achievement yielded by the Iowa Every-Pupil Basic Skills Testing Program (Grades III-VIII) for the year 1940, Stroud and Lindquist said that girls maintain a consistent and, on the whole, significant superiority over boys in all subjects tested (silent reading comprehension, work-study skills, basic language skills, and basic arithmetic skills) except arithmetic where small, insignificant differences favored boys. Discussing the possible reasons for the higher achievement of girls, Stroud and Lindquist stated that there is reason to suspect that girls experience something of a generalized feeling of inferiority with respect to their sex. Compensatory adjustments may account for their superior attainment in school. They disagree with speculation by earlier researchers that the consistent inferiority of progress and achievement in boys during their elementary school years stems from maladjustment between the boys and their teachers. Instead, Lindquist and Stroud question the practice of regarding all behavior problems in school as instances of maladjustment. Problem behavior may be little more than a method of having some fun and may be dictated to some extent by group mores. "Feminine mores do not permit as much latitude in this regard as do those of boys," said Stroud and Lindquist. "Uncooperativeness with the teacher, and a certain amount of nonchalance in doing the assignments may, like tripping a fellow-student as he perambulates down the aisle, be symptomatic of maladjustment or may be little more than instances of accepted masculine behavior."[5]

Regardless of why the norms are different for boys and girls, the fact remains that greater diversity exists within each sex than between the averages for males and females. Unless educators can place greater emphasis on the diversity than on the averages or norms, they are apt to perpetuate sex role standards for intellectual, social, and psychological performance.

Theories of Sex Role Development

Children get messages from society that encourage them to strive to live up to sex role standards. The nature of these subtle communications to children has been the subject of much discussion and theoretical formulation. Four theoretical explanations of the origin of sex roles are briefly described below: transactional analysis, identification, social reinforcement, and cognitive development.

Transactional analysis. In transactional analysis literature, stereotyped sex roles are analyzed as scripts that people learn, rehearse, and act out much like roles in a dramatic production. James and Jongeward describe a psychological script as a person's ongoing program for a life drama that dictates where the person is going with his or her life and the path that will lead there.[6] Sex role scripting in men and women causes certain parts of the personality to be developed and other parts to be suppressed. Gaps created in the personality of sex role scripted persons limit their potential to become whole human beings. In his book *Scripts People Live*, Steiner describes several variations of scripts for men and women.[7]

According to the classical scripts, men are supposed to be rational, productive, and hardworking. They are not supposed to be emotional, in touch with their feelings, or overtly loving. Women are not supposed to think rationally, be able to balance a checkbook, or be powerful. Women supply the men they relate to with the missing emotional, feeling functions, and the men take care of business for the women in their lives.

One of the goals of women's studies and of the women's movement is to create conditions that permit and assist men and women in reclaiming the full use of their personalities by freeing themselves from scripts. Spontaneity results. Transactional analysis writers hypothesize that even though people learn scripts that limit their potential, they can redecide in favor of unscripted lives. A first step in getting rid of restrictive scripts is to become aware of allegiances to particular scripts. Choosing to be free of limiting scripts, developing innate talents, and discovering real potential are the processes involved in transactional analysis.

Identification. The process through which children choose same-sex models for patterning their own behavior is referred to as identification. Children often imitate such models without conscious awareness. According to the theory of identification, sex-typed behaviors result from imitating the sex-typed behaviors of the model.

Social reinforcement. According to the social reinforcement or behavioral point of view, sex roles are developed when children are praised or discouraged for behaving in girl-like or boy-like ways. Such reinforcement may come from someone else or be self-administered. It may be vicariously experienced.[8] Praise and discouragement are important tools for the educator. If praise and discouragement are administered differentially to the two sexes, sex role socialization occurs.

Cognitive development. Cognitive development theorists explain that a child's observations of the numerous differences related to sex roles begin to form a core of meaning which is more powerful than any single observation alone or, indeed, more powerful than any particular role model alone.[9] As a child comprehends and accepts the physical reality of its sex, it is motivated to adapt to and feel competent with this reality, and to make positive evaluations about others of the same sex. It is motivated to explore the reality structure of being a member of a particular sex. It is motivated to achieve self-esteem from being a member of that sex. If a child tends to prefer a same-sex parent or teacher, this preference does not cause that child to identify itself as a member of that sex. If a child tends to imitate a same-sex parent or teacher, this imitation does not cause that child to identify itself as a member of that sex. Rather the preference and imitation result from the knowledge that it is already a member of that sex. Kohlberg states that boys, having labeled themselves as males, go on to value masculine modes because they tend to value positively the objects and acts consistent with their conceived identity. He believes that same-sex identification with adult models is less cause than consequence of natural trends of self-categorization and sex role stereotyping.

According to the cognitive development theory, children operate from organized rules about masculinity and femininity which they have induced. These inductions may be from observations of or teachings about sex-typed dress or hair styles; sex-typed actions, skills, or habits; and sex-typed toys, games, or stories. These rules, based only on the more salient sex-typed features of appearance or actions, are distortions of reality. Maccoby and Jacklin explain that children's sex role conceptions are cartoon-like—oversimplified, exaggerated, and stereotyped.[10] Children fail to note the variations in the sex role behavior of their real-life models.

To illustrate, Maccoby and Jacklin tell of a case of a four-year-old girl who insisted that girls could become nurses but only boys could become doctors, even though her own mother was a doctor. The authors point out that the child's concept was clearly not based upon imitation of a most available model. Rather it represented "an induction from instances seen and heard (in fiction as well as fact), and like most childish rule inductions it did not easily take account of exceptions."[11] Even small children acquire covert self-labels that match their biological sex. Kagan and others have observed that children assess themselves in terms of these perceived standards and label themselves depending upon how they think they conform to the set of attributes we refer to as masculine or feminine. The degree of match between their self-assessments and their understanding of the appropriate sex role standards Kagan calls *sex role identity*.[12] Consequently, children may internalize the sex role standards quite accurately, yet feel a great deal of anxiety about their sex role identity if they sense a large degree of mismatch between the two.

According to Kagan, the motivation to acquire sex-typed behavior derives from the desire to avoid or reduce this anxiety. He cites Festinger's work on cognitive dissonance to support this assertion.[13] Kagan hypothesizes that three means are available to children to avoid or reduce anxiety created by a mismatch between their own attributes and those perceived to be ideal for their gender. First, they may identify with a same-sex model and thereby come to believe that they share some of the attributes of the model. even if this is not so. Second, they may actually acquire some of the sex-typed attributes. Third, they may receive positive assurances or realistic feedback from other people that may help them make a less discrepant self-evaluation. However, Kagan is not content with these three means of avoiding or reducing children's anxiety. He suggests that the standards themselves need to be changed.

From Theory to Practice

Regardless of which theory is selected to explain how sex role stereotyped behavior occurs, the conclusion is the same. Something must be changed. The transactional analysis point of view suggests the scripts must be changed or, better yet, dropped altogether. The identification theory suggests that we provide adult models who are themselves free of sex-typed behavior. The social reinforcement theory suggests that we use praise and discouragement without differentiating on the basis of sex. And the cognitive development theory suggests that we replace the rigid standards of masculinity and femininity with a more androgynous standard.

The educator will perhaps find an eclectic approach useful. Teachers and counselors can help children see that "Boys don't cry" and "Girls aren't supposed to be good at math" are scripts that restrict behavior. Educators can strive to rid themselves of sex-typed behavior and present themselves as androgynous models for identification. They can eliminate the differential rewards and punishments or the differential praise and discouragement that have so often characterized the school setting and resulted in sex stereotyped social reinforcement. Finally, educators can use a wide array of materials, practices, policies, and procedures to decrease the influence of traditional sex role standards and replace them with a more effective model for developing human potential, the model commonly referred to in recent years as psychological androgyny.

5. A New Model

The basic question concerns not what method is best for socializing our children to meet proper sex role standards but rather what standards are appropriate. The unnecessary anxiety created in our children by socializing them to ascribe to rigid sex role standards has many side effects that we have only recently begun to acknowledge. The different emphases placed on intellectual mastery for each sex have implications for vocational choice, especially among females. Kagan recognized the limitations on intellectual growth in girls when in 1964 he stated, "Particularly well-documented is the fact that skills at problems requiring analysis and reasoning (primarily those involving spatial and mechanical reasoning, science, and mathematics) are viewed as more appropriate for boys than for girls, and girls perform less well on such tasks."[1]

Kagan, writing at a time when the educational community had not fully recognized the detrimental effects of sex role stereotyping (indeed we were then mindlessly supporting it), drew his conclusions from a review of a number of research studies. For example, he cited a 1958 study by Milton in which adolescent or adult subjects were given problems involving primarily mathematical or geometric reasoning. Females who rejected traditional feminine interests performed better on mathematical and geometric problems than those who had adopted traditional feminine behaviors.

Subject matter has come to be associated in our culture with sex role standards. Women who have chosen masculine careers, such as law, medicine, or science, may experience anxiety over their exertions in fields not traditionally feminine. Kagan observed that the typical female believes that the ability to solve problems involving geometry, physics, logic, or arithmetic is a uniquely masculine skill; and her motivation to attack such problems is low. He said this decreased involvement may reflect the fact that the girl's self-esteem is not at stake in such problems, or the fact that she is potentially threatened by the possibility that she might perform such tasks with competence. Unusual excellence on such tasks, he added, may be equated with a loss of femininity. Strong semantic associations between standards of masculinity and femininity and specific areas of knowledge have become a cause for alarm. One of the major goals of the women's movement is to change these semantic associations in the minds of children as well as adults.

Psychological Androgyny

If we can imagine women and men being encouraged to develop a full range of human qualities without the constraints of sex role stereotypes, we can begin to envision a psychologically androgynous society. In such a society behavior would be judged appropriate or inappropriate depending upon the demands of a given situation rather than upon the sex of the performer. Personality traits would be valued for their strength, effectiveness, and usefulness rather than for their associations with standards of masculinity or femininity. In a psychologically androgynous future, we may be enabled to respond appropriately to situations without weighing our behavior in advance to determine if it matches masculine or feminine stereotypes. Researcher Sandra Bem found that some people are already more androgynous than others; and her research suggests that people scoring high on her psychological androgyny scale are more likely than either masculine or feminine individuals to display sex role adaptability in a variety of situations, and to engage in situationally effective behavior without regard to sex stereotypes.[2]

Nonandrogynous sex roles can seriously restrict the range of behaviors available to individuals as they move from situation to situation, Bem said. Highly sex-typed persons, she observed, become motivated—during the course of sex role socialization—to keep their behavior consistent with internalized sex role standards. They become motivated to maintain a self-image as masculine or feminine, a goal which they presumably accomplish by suppressing any behavior that might be considered undesirable or inappropriate for their sex.

Psychological androgyny means that independence, emotionality, objectivity, competitiveness, adventurousness, and assertiveness would be as appropriate for one sex as for the other. Gentleness and sensitivity would be no more appropriate for females than

27

for males. Preparation for careers and family responsibilities would be based on individual differences, personal preferences, and innate abilities rather than sex role stereotypes. Skill in mathematics and science, ambition for a high status career, and dominance in the family structure would be no more or no less expected or socially approved in males than in females. Crying would be as acceptable or unacceptable in one sex as in the other. The situation and the individual personality would determine whether a given trait should be exhibited at any given time.

Teachers who support the concept of psychological androgyny may, for example, encourage girls as well as boys to run movie projectors, go out for track, find summer jobs, take advanced industrial arts courses, join dance bands, or become members of the science club. Teachers may help girls to understand the meaning of assertiveness and to exercise it. They may point out examples of bias in school programs, in textbooks and media, and in athletic programs as well as help students conceptualize ways in which the effects of such bias may be counteracted. Teachers, by example, may support the concept of psychological androgyny by actively seeking assignments traditionally left to the opposite sex (e.g., women teachers may take on coaching assignments, sponsorship of assembly programs, or membership on salary negotiations committees).

Teachers may find the concept of psychological androgyny quite compatible with their teaching role. Teaching often demands role behavior associated with both the traditional male and female roles: nurturance, self-reliance, cheerfulness, gentleness, forcefulness, assertiveness, understanding, warmth, independence, dominance, sensitivity, and ambition.

Fears about programming boys and girls to be alike will prove groundless. Great diversity will always exist among human beings. We seldom see two people who look or behave alike. Our fingerprints are so distinctly different they can be used as identification in criminal investigations. Just as each of us bears a unique physical appearance, each of us has a unique composite of mental and psychological potential, though some of this potential is socially desirable and some is not. Without sex stereotyping each sex would have equal access to the development of socially desirable traits.

On personality tests, socially desirable items are more likely to be selected as self-descriptive than are socially undesirable items—unless these items are associated with feminine or masculine stereotypes.[3] Not only does the feminine stereotype contain socially

undesirable items, e.g., dependence, passivity, relative in-
competence, submissiveness, and irrationality;[4] but these negative
traits also tend to be incorporated into women's self-concepts. Both
men and women associate these negative traits with stereotyped
concepts of women.[5] In a classic study of practicing mental health
clinicians that included clinical psychologists, psychiatrists, and
psychiatric social workers, mentally healthy women are described as
differing from mentally healthy men by being less independent, less
objective, less adventurous, less aggressive, less competitive, more
excitable in minor crises, more easily influenced, more submissive,
more emotional, more conceited about their appearance, and more
likely to have their feelings hurt.[6]

The study concluded with the unexpected discovery that the
standard of mental health for adults, sex unspecified, resembles the
standard for mental health in males but not in females. A double
standard of mental health existed. The general standard of health
for adults is applied to men, but women evaluated by the same standard are regarded as unhealthy. As Simone de Beauvoir's observes in
The Second Sex, "There are two kinds of people: human beings and
women. And when women start acting like human beings, they are
accused of trying to be men."[7]

Assertive Behavior Training to Promote Psychological Androgyny

When people live scripted lives, when they subscribe to rigid sex
role standards, they deny parts of themselves. They may find it
difficult to express themselves in ways that are inconsistent with
their masculine or feminine scripts. Assertive behavior training has
been used to help men and women regain control of their lives and
get in touch with their whole personalities.

People are assertive when they stand up for their legitimate
rights in such a way that the rights of others are not violated. Basic
rights of human beings are often violated unless people are aware of
such rights and know how to protect and insure them. Assertive behavior training teaches individuals how to stand up for their right to
be treated with respect; to have and express their own feelings and
opinions; to be listened to and taken seriously; to set their own
priorities; to say no without feeling guilty; to get what they pay for;
to ask for information from professionals; to make mistakes. People
are assertive when they express their wants, feelings, beliefs, and

opinions in an honest and direct way. Jakubowski has emphasized that verbal expression must be accompanied by appropriately assertive body posture, voice level, facial expression, and breathing tempo to avoid contradictory verbal messages.[8] Nonassertive behavior, frequently characterized by double messages, permits rights to be violated, either deliberately or inadvertantly. Assertive behavior does not ignore the rights of others; it does not dominate or humiliate as is characteristic of aggressive behavior.

Several writers have described ways in which assertive behavior training can be used to facilitate the growth of women. According to *The New Assertive Woman*, nonassertive behavior has traditionally been seen as an asset for women, and they have been rewarded for it; whereas the same kind of nonassertiveness in men is usually considered a distinct liability.[9] For example, for the same behaviors nonassertive women may be described with positive adjectives such as gentle, agreeable, helpful, gracious, nice, self-effacing, and nurturing; yet nonassertive men are described with negative adjectives such as milquetoast, wishy-washy, helpless, nervous, weak, a pushover, and sentimental. Aggressive men are described positively as dominating, successful, heroic, capable, strong, forceful, and manly; but aggressive women are described negatively as harsh, pushy, bitchy, domineering, obnoxious, emasculating, and uncaring.

Assertive behavior training is designed to help people change their behavior from passive to assertive rather than to aggressive. Women in particular are finding assertive behavior training helpful in reducing sex stereotyped response patterns. If young women are taught to be assertive, as they become aware of the effects of sex role stereotypes on their lives they can take steps to reduce the impact. For example, an assertive girl might volunteer more readily than a nonassertive girl to participate in stereotypically male activities at school if she is trained to identify and express her own feelings about such participation. An assertive girl might be more inclined to sign up for a physics class or an industrial arts course. She might speak up and request that sexist jokes or activities be eliminated from the classroom. She might develop interests that are not sex-typed instead of those in line with society's expectations for her, and she might choose a career in line with those interests.

Boys and men face many situations in which their activities and behaviors are restricted by sex role standards. Assertive behavior training for males can help them overcome fears associated with relaxing these strict standards in favor of the freer conditions associated with psychological androgyny.

Values Clarification and Psychological Androgyny

A value represents something important in human existence. The value we have placed on sex roles in the past has come into conflict with newer values, and students need help in understanding this conflict. In earlier times, sex roles had practical value and often lent orderliness, predictability, and ceremonial aesthetic to human interaction.[10] However, changes in technology, social organization, economics, laws, and perceptions of equality have led to a dramatic review of a most personal question: What does it mean to be a woman or a man? Present and future students will create answers to this question, answers which, as Margaret Mead has reminded us, will be different for each successive generation.[11] We can prescribe some of the answers for students today but not for our students tomorrow. At best we can help them remove the sex role question from an area of blind consent to one of informed and aware choice.

Raths, Harmin and Simon have summarized several traditional approaches for helping children develop values: (1) example setting, (2) persuasion, (3) choice limitation, (4) inspiration, (5) rules and regulations, (6) cultural or religious dogma, and (7) appeals to conscience.[12] The authors assert that these methods have been used to control behavior and to form beliefs and attitudes, but such approaches cannot lead to values that represent the free and thoughtful choice of intelligent human beings interacting with complex and changing environments. According to Raths, Harmin, and Simon, the educator who wishes to help children develop clearer values must help them (1) make free choices whenever possible, (2) search for alternatives in choice-making situations, (3) weigh the consequences of each available alternative, (4) consider what they prize and cherish, (5) affirm the things they value, (6) do something about their choices, and (7) consider and strengthen patterns in their lives. Values clarification techniques can be applied to numerous aspects of sex role stereotyping.

One method used in values clarification to stimulate student thought is the clarifying response. Without hinting what is considered good or acceptable, the teacher puts responsibility on the students to look at their behaviors or ideas and to think and decide for themselves what they want. The clarifying response is a strategy for helping students consider what they have chosen, what they prize, and what they are doing. It stimulates them to clarify their thinking and behavior and thus helps them to clarify their values.

Examples of clarifying responses cited by the authors include:

1. Are you proud of that?

2. Are you glad about that?

3. How did you feel when that happened?

4. Did you consider any alternatives?

5. When did you first begin to believe in that idea?

6. Have you thought much about that idea (or behavior)?

7. Where would that idea lead? What would be its consequences?

The teacher who is alert to sex role related comments can use clarifying responses to get students involved in discussions of their values and their underlying assumptions. Other methods for clarifying values include questionnaires, provocative statements, and passages followed by questions and group process situations.

6. Implementation

Getting There

How should women's studies K-12 be integrated into the school curriculum? Sequential arrangements are needed. Currently well-meaning teachers appear to approach feminism with similar reading lists and the same films and anecdotes that were used by last year's instructor. If some students mutter and show resistance at the beginning of a course or program, it is important to assess why they are reacting this way. Some may be expressing sexist feelings toward the subject, but others may be disappointed to be hearing a familiar story.

Integrated approaches may include direct teaching and indirect teaching and can have as much variety as the imagination will permit. Many learners demand this variety. Prekindergarten students are not ready for a lecture on the changing roles of men and women, but they can learn from illustrations that show women working outside the home and fathers cooking. The positive imagery of women should outweigh the sexist jokes, the put-downs, and the assorted developmental limitations.

Direct Teaching

Lessons built around specific behavioral objectives and concepts of women's studies are examples of direct teaching. Whole units, courses, or minicourses may be directly taught as a form of women's studies. A guest speaker may be invited to speak to a group of students on some aspect of women's studies. If the primary purpose of any activity, lesson or series of lessons is to help students better understand women's contributions to culture, and current and projected changes in women's and men's roles, it is a form of direct teaching. Any course bearing the label women's studies can be classified as direct teaching.

Direct teaching lessons appropriate for language arts and social studies classes are illustrated at elementary, intermediate, and secondary levels in *Today's Changing Roles: An Approach to Non-Sexist Teaching.*[1] The lesson plans contain procedures for helping teachers and students identify, explore, and evaluate the meaning of the changes of sex roles that are occurring. The lessons are designed to promote inquiry and are open-ended. By means of these and similar exercises, students view the world around them, interviewing and analyzing themselves and their classmates. Lesson plans in *Today's Changing Roles* are designed to raise student consciousness of sex role stereotypes in history and contemporary events, in the media and in literature, in the lives of classmates, friends, family, and in their own lives. Exercises are provided for helping the student analyze the origins and purposes of the stereotypes and evaluate the restrictions they place on people's lives. Although set answers or solutions are not presented in the illustrative lessons in *Today's Changing Roles*, students are encouraged to formulate preferred futures for themselves in relation to the stereotypes. Selected concepts from some of the lessons are grouped below by level.

Elementary

1. Male and female roles illustrated in student texts do not always reflect our lives and experiences.

2. All of us have unconscious ideas of sex role stereotypes which are often revealed in everyday conversations and situations.

3. Sex role stereotyping is often reflected in individual career choices.

4. Sex role stereotypes influence the dynamics of group interaction.

5. Self-image can perpetuate sex role stereotypes. Our self-image is determined in part by sex role stereotypes.

Intermediate

1. Conscious choices are frequently based upon unconscious acceptance of society's stereotyped ideas.

2. Society has various media which reinforce sex role stereotypes.

3. Different opinions about women's capabilities imply different roles for men.

4. Recognition of personal stereotype-based decisions, in contrast with stated beliefs, may encourage changed behavior in individuals.

5. There is a greater social acceptance of diverse capabilities and personal goals now than in the past.

6. The future will be molded by our active decisions of today.

Secondary

1. Our images of women differ from those used to describe a healthy adult.

2. Many of the rights demanded by women in 1848 and those being presently demanded are similar.

3. Sex roles influence working conditions and result in sex discrimination.

4. Sex role stereotypes can influence how future possibilities are envisioned.

5. Ridding society of sex role stereotypes will change patterns of behavior for both men and women.

6. The range of life-style choice can be broadened by the elimination of sex role stereotypes.

Direct teaching of these concepts related to women's studies may take many forms. Teachers can help students of both sexes recognize and discount sex stereotyping in books and materials which are used in their courses. As new materials appear which reflect a more equal treatment of the sexes, teachers and their students can observe whether or not balanced representation is given to women in minority cultures. A simple exercise of counting the number of pictures in a publication that are all male, all female, and mixed may be used to raise student awareness of bias. Students may make tallies of the type of activities or roles portrayed by each sex in the pictures. A teacher may call attention to the types of career models appearing in the books or ask students to speculate about the effects on young girls of the invisibility of women and the stereotyped images of those that are represented.

Students may become acquainted with research done on the extent and nature of bias in texts related to the subject being taught.

They may be asked to redesign a small portion of a text to represent more fairly and accurately the multicultural society we live in.

A short lesson in the misuse of the generic terms "man" or "he" can be taught whenever the situation arises. By suggesting possible rewordings of "Industrial Man," "Economic Man," "Man, A Course of Study," and "All men are created equal," the teachers themselves can become more aware of sexist problems in our language and, at the same time, tip off students that the next generation needs to come up with some workable solutions to such problems. Language that lives changes as needs arise. If students sense our concern over problems in the language, their search for solutions is likely to be more successful than our own capacity for dictating them. Examples of direct teaching in specific disciplinary areas are listed at the end of several of the following sections.

Indirect Teaching

Not all teaching of women's studies concepts should be direct; many powerful lessons may be indirect. When a teacher does something to promote the goals of women's studies but does not call attention to this effort, indirect teaching occurs. Indirect teaching may consist of using examples in a mathematics class of women building a house or of a boy sewing costumes for a play. Although such examples may arouse in the teacher a self-conscious reaction because of the switch from traditionally typical references to male and female role models, both teacher and students will grow accustomed to new ways of thinking about sex roles if this practice regularly occurs. In the long run indirect teaching has the advantage because it reaches toward a changed reality in the same subtle way that stereotyped reality has been promulgated. Students are less apt to pipe up with comments of, "But we had women's studies last year," and "Why do we have to do it again this year?"

Essentially, indirect teaching consists of changing some of the underlying assumptions about the sexes and their traditionally prescribed roles without making an issue of it. Indirect teaching of women's studies means adjusting some of our nonverbal signals and subtle reward and recognition systems. It means purging ourselves of sexist approaches to our subject matter and our students. It means changing our language and even occasionally our sense of humor. Indirect teaching means living it.

7.   Reading and Language Arts

One of the first textbook studies to have a major impact upon publishing companies was *Dick and Jane as Victims: Sex Stereotyping in Children's Readers.*[1] Twenty-four members of a Princeton, New Jersey, chapter of the National Organization of Women produced landmark data from 2,760 stories in 134 elementary school readers. The ratios they found were:

Boy-centered stories to girl-centered stories	5:2
Adult male main characters to adult female main characters	3:1
Male biographies to female biographies	6:1
Male animal stories to female animal stories	2:1
Male folk or fantasy stories to female folk or fantasy stories	4:1

Women on Words and Images, as the women called themselves, examined the images of males and females presented to youngsters, the mirrors held up to young readers for reference as they build their own characters.

Young males not only appeared more often in the stories than females, but they also enjoyed far richer experiences—except those which involved the display of emotions. They explored for treasure, wrestled alligators, helped apprehend burglars, endured pain, rescued animals, earned money, constructed complex apparatuses, and solved challenging problems. Often the male succeeded in the stories at the expense of a passive, naive female whose chief function was to serve as a foil and audiovisual aid for the clever boy. Although the action of the male child had virtually no limits, the female was much more closely circumscribed. Especially in the psychomotor domain, the male appeared to enjoy a wider range of activity. Confident boys were pictured in situations making faces, accomplishing difficult feats of agility, and using a full range of motion. By contrast, girls appeared in restricted physical activities such as playing jacks or hopscotch, and their range of motion was limited as well. Often their hands were shown folded in their laps or hidden behind their backs.

Dick and Jane as Victims was not the first analysis of role-limiting pictures of females, but it was one of the first to be widely viewed, studied, and copied. Following publication of this book, some textbook companies revised their guidelines to reduce if not eliminate sexist content.

Though the educator may acknowledge the element of unfairness in sex stereotyped literature and reading texts, does differential treatment favoring male characters in the books make any behavioral difference? Are we really limiting the futures of our children because of the traditional stories and illustrations? After all, the Title IX regulations do not require the elimination of sex stereotyped books. McArthur and Eisen assessed the effects on achievement behavior.[2] They found that boys persisted longer on a task after hearing a story about a male achiever than after a story depicting the same behavior in a female. A trend in the opposite direction was also observed in girls. The images boys and girls see in books do make a difference in their motivation and performance in the classroom, though females may be a bit more persistent under adverse conditions than males.

Direct Teaching

- Develop classroom activities around identifying bias found in television, textbooks, movies, library books, and magazines.

- Encourage teachers and students to ask themselves consciousness-raising questions. If they cannot name five American women writers, ask them why not. Is it because they have concluded that the writers were not worth remembering? Is it because the writers were omitted from anthologies and libraries? Did their teachers fail to make the women writers come alive?

- Encourage students to ask divergent questions about traditional literary works. What concepts of women does an author suggest by leaving them out? Critical readers should want to know more about Rip Van Winkle's nagging wife who raised the children alone while her husband went bowling and hunting and took long naps.[3]

Indirect Teaching

- Identify how textbooks are selected in your community. Write to and meet with persons responsible for textbook selection at local and state levels to voice your concerns. Urge the purchase of quality materials and inclusions of supplementary materials.

- When new anthologies are selected that are supposedly free of sexist bias, examine them carefully. Should the elimination of sexist bias extend beyond the selection of literary passages and include the accompanying literary criticism? We think so.

- When new books are selected that are comparatively free of sexist bias, consider their effect. Will they be used in the lower grades while the upper grades are permitted to maintain their sexist books upon the premise that subject content is somehow protected by academic freedom? We think instructors at all levels should reexamine the biases of the books likely to be used in their courses.

8.   Social Studies

One of the earliest feminist analyses of social studies was an article by Janice Law Trecker, "Women in U.S. History High-School Textbooks," which appeared in *Social Education*.[1] It deserves rereading. Although she found scanty representation of women in her sample, Trecker peered far beyond headcounting. She found that women's accomplishments were not fully acknowledged. Anne Hutchinson, for example, was viewed as second best to Roger Williams. Women abolitionists were seldom quoted. Where were the words of Sojourner Truth?

The handicaps that women faced in early America have been emphasized but their efforts in their own behalf minimized. Men were portrayed as the protectors, yet Trecker noted that women were much more active in court defenses of their rights than textbooks admitted.

Women were there, too, in the Revolutionary War, the Civil War, and the World Wars. But again their contributions were minimized by the textbooks which Trecker studied. The books lacked the viewpoint of a William H. Chafe with his updated *The American Woman* and the sociology of Betty Friedan's *The Feminine Mystique*.[2,3]

The position of women in traditional history texts is analogous to that of blacks in earlier works. For George Washington Carver and the peanut, substitute Marie Curie and radium. But Curie had an additional classification that clouds the perspective of the historian: her identity was defined in relation to her husband.

It is tempting to select women such as Dolley Madison or Martha Washington, who were associated with famous men, and simply give them more coverage. But women's situations are often complex. When the New York women's group gave Woodrow Wilson the Fourteen Points, how much rewriting did he do? How much was his contribution? For the DNA discoveries, how great a debt do Watson and Crich owe to the late woman scientist, Rosalind Franklin, whose name already seems to be increasingly forgotten? In education, let us remember that it is Jacobson and Rosenthal who have given us the Pygmalion-in-the-classroom effect.

It is no less important to write about the women in history who were independent of prominent colleagues or spouses. Sybil Ludington rode as harrowing a ride as Paul Revere to warn the colonists, yet Revere's horse receives more attention than Ludington.

One of the ultimate problems for the social scientist is gaining a raised and altered consciousness of what women have done and what they are capable of accomplishing. It is popular to interpret events in terms of yang and yin, masculine and feminine. History and political science have frequently been written from the "drum and trumpets" angle with just an occasional salacious "bedsprings and strumpets" tidbit thrown in. Men are shown as the principal characters on the hilltops of the yang chapters, but women appear in the quiet yin valleys. Even de Beauvoir seems to assume that the hilltop eras were dominated by famous men. Questions to consider are: Were there no prominent women in the yang periods, too? Will we remember Indira Gandhi, Margaret Thatcher, and Golda Meir? Or will the late 1960's and early 1970's precipitate as the Henry Kissinger era?

Direct Teaching Suggestions

- Use a multitext approach. Compare several accounts of a woman's contributions.

- Try a simulation such as *Herstory* and *Puzzle* by Interact.[4] Examine a variety of women's roles in a sociology unit.

- Bring a visitor from a foreign country during the geography period. Examine some of the stereotypes about woman's place that look picturesque and static in the textbooks but that in reality are changing.

- Identify and analyze cultural blocks that inhibit the development of women's abilities.

- Compare the problems faced by women with the problems faced by other minorities. Note Gunnar Myrdal or Shirley Chisholm, for example.

Indirect Teaching Suggestions

- Build a futuristic society with altered roles among the inhabitants.

- Organize a team teaching approach to a humanities class with each member responsible for a different aspect of feminism.

- Have the students write their own feminist textbook.

41

9. Mathematics

Maccoby and Jacklin have concluded that the two sexes are similar in their early acquisition of quantitative concepts and their mastery of arithmetic in grade school.[1] Girls learn to count at an earlier age; but through the elementary school years there are no consistent sex differences in skill at arithmetical computation.[2] However, when boys reach age 12 or 13, their mathematical skills begin to increase faster.[3] In high school boys excel in arithmetical reasoning fairly consistently, and this trend continues into college and adulthood.[4]

Several researchers have begun to suggest that sex role stereotypes may account for some, if not all, of the sex differences in mathematical performance. Consider for a moment the systematic analysis of grade school mathematics textbooks by Weitzman and Rizzo.[5] Mathematics textbooks show males as mathematically competent but show some females as having difficulty with simple addition and being baffled by counting. Weitzman and Rizzo found stereotypes in math problems: adult women divide pies and shop. Other math problems were found in which girls were paid less than boys for the same work. Sex is used frequently as a category for dividing people. For example, Weitzman and Rizzo's study revealed that when the textbooks explain set theory, girls are classified as people who sew and cry. "When sex is used as a category, girls are told that they can be classified as different—as typically emotional or domestic." Although not limited to mathematics textbooks, "dumb girl" images and the portrayal of adult women as mathematically incompetent contribute to the stereotype that math is for boys.

Fennema and Sherman have found that sex role stereotyping affects attitudes and proficiency in mathematics from the early years onward. Peers, parents, and the girl herself eventually build the image of a "female head that's not much for figures."[6] Fennema and Sherman blame sex role stereotyping for the tendency of fewer girls than boys to choose mathematics courses after the second year in high school.

Mathematics appears as a prerequisite subject in the career ladders of a variety of professions in which women are poorly represented. Three years of high school mathematics are often required for introductory college chemistry; calculus is required for most college physics courses. Sells refers to the lack of adequate preparation in high school mathematics as a "critical filter" in cutting down the percentage of women in many fields other than mathematics. She examined a sample of freshmen admitted at the University of California, Berkeley in the fall of 1972 and found that 57 percent of the boys had taken four full years of mathematics including the trigonometry–solid geometry sequence compared with 8 percent of the girls. According to Sells, the four-year mathematics sequence is required for admission to Mathematics 1A, a course required for majoring in every field at the university except the humanities, the social sciences, librarianship, social welfare, and education which are fields where female representation has been strong.

One of the basic recommendations of the 1973 Carnegie Commission on Higher Education said, ". . . high school counselors and teachers should encourage women who aspire to professional careers to choose appropriate educational programs. They should also encourage them to pursue mathematical studies throughout high school, because of the increasing importance of mathematics as a background, not only in engineering and the natural sciences, but also in other fields, such as the social sciences and business administration."[8]

What can the mathematics teacher do to support the women's studies effort of the school? Luchins found teachers to be more influential than friends or parents in encouraging girls in mathematics in school. Teachers can work to improve young women's attitudes towards mathematics and help them overcome "mathophobia" or math anxiety, a problem which seems to be greater for girls than boys.[9]

The father's encouragements and expectations—or lack of them—for his daughter in math are suggested background factors. Ernest and others asked students from which parent they got help in homework. For both sexes the mothers helped more than the fathers until the higher grades, when a shift occurred in mathematics. By grade 7 the fathers had taken over dramatically in math homework help. Probably as many mothers need to gain self-assurance in approaching mathematics as fathers need to realize that their daughters could use nurturance in this subject.

New programs to counteract math anxiety are appearing in the form of workshops and course revisions. "Math for Girls" is an eight-week, discovery-oriented course for 6- to 14-year-olds, conducted by Nancy Kreinberg and Rita Liff (Lawrence Hall of Science, University of California, Berkeley, California 94720). Mills College (Oakland, California 94613) conducted math and science workshops for young women in grades 7 through 12 during October 1976. A "Discovery Course in Elementary Mathematics and Its Applications" is part of a pilot program directed by Alice Shafer (Mathematics Department, Wellesley College, Wellesley, Massachusetts 02181) that aims to develop new models for teaching math.[10]

In the absence of textbooks free of sex role stereotypes, teachers and counselors can help students look for and learn to recognize bias and important omissions in books. They can ask students to speculate on the effects of such stereotypes on girls, and help young girls to understand the importance of a strong mathematics background in keeping career options open. They can explain the sequential nature of courses in mathematics and the relationship between high school preparation and college options.

Direct Teaching

- Make greater efforts to recruit girls in mathematics courses in the tenth and later grades.

- Sponsor math anxiety workshops for teachers, parents, and students.

Indirect Teaching

- Examine math story problems and illustrations for evidence of sex stereotyping. Look for materials in which males are portrayed as the chief problem-solvers as well as for materials in which girls are relegated to the task of solving arithmetical problems only within the domestic scene.

- Encourage mothers and young women to help tutor students with their math homework.

- Prepare story problems where sex role stereotyped activities are reversed (i.e., show boys baking cookies).

- Display a picture of a famous woman mathematician such as Emmy Noether.

10.   Science

Science has been sex-typed as a masculine domain in the school curriculum. Yet sequential preparation in science is necessary for postsecondary education aimed at jobs in scientific and technical areas. Unless girls are encouraged to overcome the stereotypes associated with the study of science, they may unthinkingly close career doors for themselves before they reach high school. The concentration of women workers in a limited number of occupations, frequently in low-paying, dead-end jobs, is evidence enough that the numerous careers related to science are inadequately explored by female youth. In 1973 women made up 99 percent of the secretaries, 96 percent of the nurses, 83 percent of the librarians, and 70 percent of the school teachers—but only 22 percent of the accountants and less than 1 percent of the engineers. The trend is not different among younger people. In 1971 women were still being awarded only 12 percent of the degrees in architecture and environmental design, 14 percent of the degrees in the physical sciences, and 1 percent of the degrees in engineering. Percentages of doctoral degrees granted to women in the sciences were higher in the 1920's than in any decade since.[1] The proportion of women in science careers continues to be small. The level of degree, salary, academic rank, and administrative responsibility increases as the proportion of women declines.

"But I don't like science," a girl is often heard to say. Is she aware that her interests have been subtly programmed and sex-typed for her? Is she aware that her elementary science textbooks contained approximately 75 percent male illustrations? Does she realize that only 6 percent of the science textbook illustrations showed adult women?[2] Typically, the girl interested in science has been encouraged to consider nursing.

A science teacher may wonder what effect she or he may have on the young female. A 1976 nationwide study of barriers to the consideration of careers in science reports that extra encouragement from teachers is one of the three most important factors in explaining why some girls do seriously consider science careers. The other two factors are (1) knowledge that attitudes are changing about what is appropriate work for women, and (2) encouragement from family to fulfill individual potential.[3]

Direct Teaching

• Present information about women who have careers in science and technology.[4]

• Help girls to understand the effects of sex-stereotyping and bias in science and career materials on their perceptions and science-related interests.

• Provide information about contributions of women in science, other than the familiar Marie Curie.

• Explain the U.S. Department of Labor projections for science and engineering careers for the next decade.[5]

• Relate the changing roles of men and women to the career potential for women in science.

Indirect Teaching

• Select materials that avoid sex stereotypes in their illustrations (e.g., with pictures in which women are actively engaged in science, outdoors as well as indoors, and in which as many men are looking over women's shoulders as vice versa).

• Invite women scientists into the classroom to talk about relevant topics.

• Encourage girls to enter science fairs, to participate actively in science assemblies, and to display their work.

• Encourage girls to develop manipulative hobbies, such as constructing models and radios.

• Encourage girls to participate in Christmas census bird counts, rock climbs, spelunking, and scuba diving.

11.   Sports and Physical Education

Many long-overdue changes are occurring in the field of sports and physical education as a result of Title IX and the feminist movement.

A gradual but significant change has occurred in the purpose underlying various sports. Because some intercollegiate sports have evolved into multimillion dollar enterprises, and because interscholastic school teams have developed into junior copies of intercollegiate sports, women and men physical educators have been arguing for another form of sports. They have sought an alternative form of psychomotor activity closer to the club and intramural model than to the interscholastic mode. Since the very motive for play often differs from the interscholastic to the intramural games, the new model is being used to encourage all students to participate. Even the interscholastic sports supporters have been pressured into paying lip service to this ideal. Under the old interscholastic model, school patrons applauded the gifted few, stressed winning, and sought monetary profit. The newer alternative intramural club model of women encourages games for the sake of socialization and play.

Another change involves the scope of physical activities. Title IX was designed to increase equitable opportunities for the sexes in sports, but it exempted institutions from providing body contact sports for women. However, body contact sports for women are becoming more popular as both segregated and coeducational activities. Among intramural programs, coeducational volleyball and flag and touch football appear to be more popular than ever in the United States, and women's soccer is on the increase in Western Europe.

The ancient assumption that women are physiologically inferior to men has been challenged by these changes. New research is appearing, and physical educators are making better use of older data from physiology. The answer is not yet at hand to tell us what women (and men) are capable of performing. Endurance comparisons between the sexes indicate levels of performance are much closer than previously thought, due in part to more women participants. When a mark falls in women's track and field, the difference between the old and new women's records is often greater than the difference between men's and women's records. The line of ascending performance for women appears to be sharper, and the differences in level of performance are drawing closer.

But as we reduce the physical separation of the sexes in most of the programs, we may overlook psychological separateness. In the day-to-day practices of the classroom and the playground, we find subtle classifications of we-they which prevent our entering an era of psychological androgyny in physical education. It is so easy to assign to boys the task of rolling up the mats and arranging the heavy equipment while the girls are handing out the jerseys. It seems so natural for a teacher to expect girls to have whiter socks and cleaner uniforms than boys. If we persist in maintaining one set of expectations for men and another for women, it seems unlikely that we will be able to diagnose individual differences.

The we-they expectation soon yields a double standard of action. A careless teacher will walk daily past the trophy case that honors the accomplishments of the boys' teams but that offers only a few slight testimonials to the physical history of the girls. In the physical education class, the teacher may find a noisy group of boys who ask to play an organized team sport. The less assertive girls may be left to follow quieter pursuits. And the teacher may unconsciously choose to supervise the more visible sport, the boys' activity, for which there will be still more trophies and public acclaim.

Some teachers perceive sex role socialization problems more quickly than others. Berkeley, California, teachers observed that playground play varied distinctly between boys and girls. During a typical recess, the boys organized a vigorous, competitive game of kickball while the girls engaged in jungle gym and other unstructured play. The teacher discussed the reasons for the difference in playground behavior with the students. "The girls don't know how to kick," one boy said. A girl admitted that she did not know how to kick well, but added, "I'd like to learn." After the students and teachers became aware of the problem, they took steps to see that both sexes enjoyed a greater range of physical experiences. The girls soon lined up for kicking practice.

To move into an era of psychological androgyny, teachers will have to become aware of themselves physically. If they possess poor physical self-images, it seems unlikely that they will know what their own capabilities are for physical movement and skills. More important, we doubt that they can help students in physical development without self-knowledge and pride of their own. New "survival consciousness" workshops for teachers may answer part of this assumed need. A second step may be the design and use of personal fitness programs.

One last implementation suggestion for physical educators and administrators is that the educators include more class discussions in their courses. In too many instances, physical education class discussions have consisted either of terse chalk talks or else have featured the teacher exhorting students to become better citizens. There is a need for discussions involving psychological and sociological aspects of sports. Sex stereotyping is one important topic which should be addressed. Why do some coaches pressure young women athletes to avoid dating during a particular athletic season? Why do parietal rules differ for male and female athletes on trips? Why have some males experienced difficulty accepting women competitors in sports such as football and horse racing? We suspect that males who have such difficulties are grown versions of the boys who once did not invite the girls to play kickball.

Title IX has attempted to eliminate sex segregation in many sports and, except for some aspects of sex education, in physical education. (Separate locker rooms have been maintained because of rights of privacy.) The "separate but equal" doctrine has not been entirely rejected by the interpreters of Title IX in the schools. A subdoctrine has appeared in the adjective "equitable." The boys may have wrestling teams, but the girls are offered gymnastics or field hockey. Is that an equitable arrangement? Is it equitable to offer softball for girls in the fall and again in the following late spring-to-summer and count it as two sports? Is it fair that the boys are denied the opportunity to enroll in a self-defense unit?

Across-the-board answers are impossible. But surely we may seek solutions to many of these questions under three broad ideals: (1) providing a physical education program which introduces youngsters to a variety of individual and team sports, (2) recognizing individual differences and helping all students to find success experiences, and (3) encouraging considerable freedom of choice in the later grades. Elementary physical education should provide a broad range of exploratory activities. Secondary physical education should experiment more with combinations of team and individual sports based more heavily upon student choice and individual differences. Both sexes should explore wrestling and field hockey.

Self-defense for women brings up a transitional problem. Is it wise to offer such a separate course for young women? At this point in time women need more help in developing physical self-confidence than men do. The physical discrepancy is analogous to assertiveness in discussions. Just a feminists feel that women temporarily need consciousness raising and assertive behavior training groups, they also feel self-defense classes have a useful function.[1] Women need to increase their overall physical survival skills so they do not have to feel dependent upon or intimidated by men.

Direct Teaching

- Provide coeducational physical education experiences in fitness programs, competitive sports, intramural and club activities, and recreation.

- Provide success experiences for boys and girls in physical education. Devise means of overcoming skill deficits.

- Discuss problems of sex role stereotyping with classes. Encourage boys and girls to arrange heavy equipment, act as judges, and take part in a full array of activities.

Indirect Teaching

- Recruit students of both sexes for athletic teams.

- Show concern for the skill development of boys and girls. Avoid the unconscious supervisory practice of drifting over to the highly skilled group and giving the greatest attention to the gifted athletes.

- Encourage women faculty to earn coaching certification and to sponsor recreational activities for girls.

12. Fine Arts

It is all too easy for students to assume that there are no notable women artists and musicians. Few school libraries contain useful books which counteract the impression that women are only to be painted and to have compositions dedicated to them by men. In colleges, syllabi from art and music history courses are often crowded with male representatives.

But there is much more to the story of women in the fine arts. Many women produced great works. Occasionally they appeared with a more famous man: Suzanne Valadon with her son Utrillo; Sarah Peale with her illustrious uncle and cousins; Wilhelmina and Anna Amalia, the sisters of Frederick the Great; Clara Wieck, who married Robert Schumann; and Fanny Mendelssohn Hensel, the sister of Felix. More often the women artists carved out enduring reputations through their own talents. Women prodigies such as the painters Artemisia Gentileschi and Elisabeth Vigée-Lebrun and the composers Francesca Caccini and Alice Mary Smith deserve to be represented and studied in survey courses. Some of the names mentioned in association with men actually enjoyed greater reputations in their own day than the men. Clara Wieck was an example. Before her marriage, she composed a number of works and gave successful concerts in Vienna, Weimar, Copenhagen, St. Petersburg, and

Moscow besides being named court pianist to the Austrian emperor. Schumann became known as "the artist's husband."

If there were so many women in the fine arts, why do our schools remain silent on their contributions? Sophie Drinker has written an anthropological explanation which deserves careful study.[1] In some ages, such as the Golden Period of Greece, women's contributions were welcomed. Sappho may well have been to music and poetry what Pericles was to sculpture.

Later, tribal and religious taboos effectively cut women off from easily producing music. Those taboos help to explain the repression of women composers by Sibelius, Mendelssohn's opposition to his own sister's efforts to publish her works, Sir Thomas Beecham's derisive comments about women musicians, and the many refusals of music faculties to admit brilliant women students even when those prospective students had won outstanding prizes with their compositions. Those taboos have been reinforced also by other social forces, such as male control of patronage and the fine arts press.

Finally, some women artists and musicians sublimated a significant portion of their creative energies into the role of mother and wife. Clara Wieck provides a useful illustration. Wieck found herself a widow with seven children at the age of thirty-five. In order to survive, she spent more time giving concerts and teaching than she did composing. In her mature years she did not command an office of leadership that allowed her to compose. From her sense of self-sacrifice and compassion, she spent her energies popularizing Beethoven's and Schumann's works and nurturing Brahms; and her own development languished.

Direct Teaching

- Make use of elementary music materials that do not give sex stereotyped roles to the students, such as *The Grange Song Book*.

- Demonstrate to your students the possibilities of new themes in art vis-à-vis the feminist art movements in New York and California in 1969 and the early 1970's. One example is the Womanspace exhibition house directed by Judy Chicago. (See her book: *Through the Flower: My Struggle as a Woman Artist*. New York: Doubleday, 1975.)

- Invite local women artists, musicians, and artisans to your class.

- Build female role exemplars for your students.

Indirect Teaching

- Add to your library collection works which will help students appreciate great women artists and composers. Eleanor Tufts' *Our Hidden Heritage: Five Centuries of Women Artists* (New York: Paddington Press, Ltd., 1974) and Sophie Drinker's *Music and Women, The Story of Women in Their Relation to Music* (New York: Coward-McCann, Inc., 1948) are indispensable works. A two-volume LP, "Woman's Work" (Gemini Hall Records RAP 1010), contains the music of some outstanding post-Renaissance, western women composers.

- Find a copy of the Venezuelan national anthem (composed by Teresa Carreño).

- Ask the music teacher to have an occasional student-conductor day when both boys and girls can be asked to try out the leadership experience.

- Encourage students of both sexes to compose.

- Recognize the birthdays of famous women artists and composers.

13. Home Economics

Home economics educators have felt for years that their subject suffered from the inadequate image of "cooking and sewing only." Students and the public too often have missed the larger possibilities in this field.

Interpersonal relations have been stressed by home economics educators as an area badly in need of greater attention. Problems of sex role stereotyping offer large possibilities for the enrichment of class discussions. A teacher may ask students to describe several kinds of relationships between the sexes. Students may choose characters from literature, from television, and from people they know. Students may learn to diagnose relationships by means of simple oppositions: love–hate, strong–weak; rich–poor. After the short diagnoses, students may study other concepts of relationships between the sexes and make longer diagnoses. *Masculine/Feminine,* a book of readings edited by Betty Roszak and Theodore Roszak, contains several useful essays.[1] One example is "Women as a Minority Group," by Helen Mayer Hacker. Hacker observes an economic basis behind the relations between the sexes. Because the industrial revolution made men recognize women as competitors for jobs, intense efforts were made to drive women away from the marketplace.

Since the days of the suffragettes, the relations between the sexes have been characterized by a type of opposition intermediate between competition and outright conflict. Hacker calls this intermediate type of opposition "contravention." Contravention occurs when couples bicker or snipe at each other instead of resolving their conflict. The sarcastic fantasies of James Thurber assume a new importance when they are viewed against Hacker's theoretical background. The home economics teacher who wishes to move into the era of psychological androgyny must help young people reshape marital relationships to avoid contravention. The replacement of competition by cooperation would be a good first step. Probably even more important is the avoidance of comparisons based upon sexual classification.

54

Home economics teachers may want to relate the concept of futurism to married and single life-styles. What would an ideal marriage consist of? What are the advantages and disadvantages of single life or married life? Jessie Bernard has devoted a large amount of research to a variety of American marital practices in her book, *The Future of Marriage*. Bernard's search for various marital forms even included science fiction. She mentions Poul Anderson's *Virgin Planet* in which there are three types of marriage. For the male the first marriage was to satisfy sexual urges, the second was for reproduction of the species, and the third was for mature companionship. The sequence was arranged differently (by this male writer) for women: the first marriage was for reproduction of the species, the second was to satisfy sexual urges, and the third was for companionship.[2]

Home economics courses may include studies of factors that cement and maintain successful marriages or that yield strongly independent or interdependent life-styles. A 1975–76 study of over 4,000 Ohio high school students revealed that one of their chief concerns was the break up of families, yet this subject ranked as one of the least frequently taught in their schools.[3]

Feminist views can also enrich a home economics curriculum by relating homemaking and career roles. The career education movement calls for the classroom teacher to have a richer acquaintance and a more intimate tie with the industrial world. Elizabeth Simpson notes that the traditional home economics teacher lacks personal experience with the careers that are outside of education.[4]

Direct Teaching

- Hold discussions about sex discrimination and feminism. Invite a feminist speaker to assist with the class discussions.

- Examine a variety of life-styles among various classes and cultures. Study patriarchal, shared, and matriarchal examples. Examine nuclear, single-parent, and extended-family patterns.

- Encourage students of both sexes to develop homemaking skills.

- Study causes of divorce and reasons for successful marriages.

- Relate nutrition to health and longevity. Examine the correlates of stress and life expectancy in males and the ways in which diet may combat the effects of stress.

Indirect Teaching

- Recruit boys and girls to advanced elective courses in home economics, and require coeducational home economics in the junior high–middle school years.

- Work closely with the business community. Build options in the minds of the students for a variety of careers. Demonstrate the applications of home economics to such occupations as chef, food inspector, journalist, buyer, and advertiser.

- Develop a greater understanding of women's current and future participation in the work force. Encourage girls and boys to explore nontraditional career models.

14. Foreign Language

Many of the sexist concerns of the social studies and English teachers are applicable to the work of the foreign language instructor. Yet at least three factors combine to create some special concerns for foreign language instruction.

The first of these factors is the increasing pressure for revision of sexist textbooks. Some older texts still have cartoons that depict women as little more than sex objects, and they often have a picaresque structure using, for example, a boy from the United States and his brother going on a trip with their father. Stereotypes abound, and there are suggestions of elitism. The focus is from outside the new country in. Newer approaches have fewer stereotypes and present the culture from inside the country out.

The second factor is that of gender. Spanish, French, and German, the foreign languages most American students study, exhibit more differentiation of nouns, pronouns, and adjectives by sex than English does. For example, *they* is neuter in English, but not in Spanish and Portuguese. If a crowd contains 99 women and one man, the pronoun *they* still is masculine. Many American beginning foreign language students are pubescent; and perhaps this changing phase in their lives accounts in part for their curiosity over gender in a new language. Teachers sometimes exploit this interest when they see it aroused, so that a virtual "sex trip" occurs. But there are other ways to approach the teaching of gender which may produce a healthier attitude in students.

The third factor that affects sexism in foreign language instruction involves ethnocentrism, feminism, and the other culture. Although some educators claim that they have rid themselves of ethnocentrism, no one escapes entirely. It seems only natural that foreign language teachers should develop a passion for the language and culture of a given country. The problem arises over the degree to which the teacher should unquestioningly accept a sexist practice from that other culture.

An example from Japanese may illustrate the problem. It is said to be customary in conversation to refer to a husband but not to a wife, for ". . . a wife is not considered worthy of mention or is to be kept private."[1] How should a feminist foreign language teacher approach or avoid such an example? Some anthropological purists might argue that the practice should be passed on to students as is, because any variation would represent a foreign intrusion. Possibly the test of whether to accept a sexist practice in a language might be to substitute racism or cannibalism. Would we be satisfied with leaving those practices *in situ* without suggesting any alternatives?

Direct Teaching

- Examine current foreign magazine articles for evidence of feminist interest and alternatives to the older sex role stereotypes.

- Collect samples of foreign feminist journals, such as the Swedish *Hertha*.

- Help the students understand the ways in which languages contribute to sex role stereotyping and the ways in which this problem is being corrected.

- In order to place the *machismo* problem in perspective, mention the presence of matriarchal villages and areas within larger societies.

- Use vowel harmony as a means of introducing the concept of gender rather than sexuality. In many instances, the teacher can say, "Listen to the endings." As another alternative, the teacher may speak of classes of nouns.

Indirect Teaching

- Interview a variety of guests who have travelled in the country under study.

- Maintain a varied, up-to-date collection of magazines, books, newspapers, and other artifacts from the country.

- Mention important women in the foreign culture such as Gabriela Mistral, the Nobel-Prize-winning poet from Chile; or Catherine the Great of Russia.

15. Industrial and Vocational Education

If we examine the basic goals of industrial arts as stated in 1968 by the American Vocational Association Revision Committee, we find five goals, all revolving around the individual and the industrial society in which he or she lives. These are:

1. To develop an insight and understanding of industry and its place in our culture.

2. To discover and develop talents, aptitudes, interests, and potentialities of individuals for technical pursuits and applied sciences.

3. To develop an understanding of industrial processes and the practical application of scientific principles.

4. To develop basic skills in the proper use of common industrial tools, machines, and processes.

5. To develop problem-solving and creative abilities involving the materials, processes, and products of industry.[1]

These goals appear to be equally significant for young men and women. In 1976 the NEA assembled a Bicentennial Panel that re-examined the Cardinal Principles of 1918.[2] The Panel's views resembled the goals expressed above, and are important for boys and girls.

However, translating three worthy goals into common experiences for both sexes remains a major problem. The Title IX amendments have made the problem a pressing issue.

Junior high and middle schools have discovered that it is easy to correct the channeling which formerly sent boys through industrial arts and girls into home economics. If the subjects are required, they should be taken by both sexes. The simplicity of the schedule changes which mix the sexes contrasts sharply with the rigidity of the sex discrimination that kept them apart for decades.

But in the high school the task of eradicating sex discrimination enrollments in the practical arts is not so easy. Future plans that include marriage, military service, college, and other post-secondary educational work intervene and often split students up into dozens of electives. Sex stereotyped attitudes reinforce the course choices. Disproportionate numbers of girls are found in secretarial-related studies, and a preponderance of boys are in vocational agriculture.

Direct Teaching

- Include consciousness-raising activities in the conferences and workshops for industrial educators. Consider why some industrial educators resist having girls as students and others welcome them. Examine career education materials for evidence of sex stereotyping. Make alternative materials available that present a fair treatment of the sexes.

- Recruit promising students and teachers of both sexes to practical arts programs. Encourage women teachers in industrial arts and vocational agriculture to appear as role examplars so that they can attract larger numbers of female students.

- Discuss the sexist practices that students encounter at their off-campus work stations in distributive education classes.

- Discuss the effects of changes in technology on the functional relevance of traditional sex roles.

Indirect Teaching

- Experiment with new electives and minicourses in practical arts classes in order to achieve a more balanced enrollment. Horticulture electives, for example, have appealed to both sexes.

- Invite adult exemplars of both sexes to the classroom as resource speakers.

- Include equitable numbers of men and women business representatives to serve on career education advisory committees.

- Apply lessons and activities in futurism to a number of the practical arts. Such learning experiences could include an examination of present and projected sex roles.

16. Counseling

Counselors and teachers can help each other develop sensitivities to sex role stereotyping and work toward its elimination. School counselors may be able to serve as a catalyst for change in classrooms as well as in the counseling office. For example, they may use small group guidance sessions for both sexes to engage in consciousness raising, assertive behavior training, values clarification, career guidance, and family life planning. If teachers are kept informed of the rationale for such activities, they may work cooperatively to plan and coordinate parallel and follow-up activities for the classroom. Counselors, working cooperatively with faculty, may be able to develop in-service programs related to the need for integrated approaches to women's studies. Many of the ways for contributing to women's studies programs in schools are identified in the growing body of literature on nonsexist counseling.

The counseling office should work closely with the Title IX coordinator in each school system to insure that discrimination in educational programs or activities is eliminated and prevented from recurring. School districts receiving federal money are required by Title IX to appoint a coordinator and to issue policy statements on district commitment to eliminate sex discrimination in employment and educational programs. Counselors should help interpret these policies to students and to other school personnel. The U.S. Office of Education has issued materials for helping districts comply with Title IX.[1] In 1973 Cook and Stone urged that in every educational institution there be at least one place where female students and staff could bring their concerns with confidence and faith that their concerns would be viewed seriously and handled fairly.[2] Title IX requires that students be made aware of nondiscriminatory policies. As students become aware of these policies, they may become more sensitive to sexist practices with the result that the counselor will be needed as a women's advocate.

To become fully aware of discriminatory counseling practices uncovered by researchers, and to plan strategies for eliminating the detrimental effects of sex role stereotyping, counselors should establish a basic resource file. The resource file may be used with or by students, staff, and community members. Help in establishing such a file can be obtained from the American Personnel and Guidance Association's Sex Equality in Guidance Opportunities Project (SEGO) (1607 New Hampshire Avenue, N.W., Washington, D.C. 20009). The SEGO Project represents a coordinated national effort to provide technical assistance to elementary and secondary school counselors and related educational personnel so that they may recognize and change the detrimental and limiting effects of the sex role stereotyping which prevents children from developing and utilizing their full capabilities.[3] Among the SEGO materials is a list of State Trainers in each state and the District of Columbia. Multimedia kits have been developed by the Project for State Trainers to use for display and discussion in local workshops.

Another important resource for the school counselors' file is *Sex Fairness in Career Guidance: A Learning Kit,* a set of materials developed under a contract from the National Institute of Education.[4] Included are discussions of traditional family and occupational roles for both sexes, an introduction to a sex-fair guidance program, an annotated resource guide to readings, and other audiovisual material. The counselor may wish to share this kit with teachers, administrators, and librarians.

Counselors should cooperate with teachers in conducting career workshops for women students for many reasons. Young women show a decreasing interest in expressing career choices after their junior high years.[5] Girls are found in disproportionate numbers in certain secondary school subjects such as typing and shorthand, and their practical arts experiences appear to acquaint them with only a limited range of career choices. Until recently females were excluded from significant vocational schools and career programs such as the chefs' schools. Even now their numbers are small in the prestigious trade, technical, and industrial education curriculums.

It is not secret that certain high status professions such as medicine, dentistry, engineering, and law have few women representatives. Though science and mathematics are essential in some of these fields, women graduate from high school with inadequate attitudes toward and background in these subjects. As we noted earlier, girls tend to associate those four fields with the male sex.

Young women need career education programs which will help lessen such difficulties and limitations. They need more than larger representation in certain classes and fields, however. In the period of transition to psychological androgyny, special help will be required to furnish women with the self-confidence to succeed in new careers. Women must be helped to discover the various and intricate rules and practices within their desired careers. Gaining entry is not enough; women must also learn about the pitfalls and promises.

The concept that "actions speak louder than words" applies clearly to women's studies. For example, career leaflets selected for display in the guidance office may go a long way toward either supporting other nonsexist messages from counselors or in contradicting them. Any materials not written with the explicit intention of including wider options for women are likely to be counterproductive. Boys as well as girls should see career materials portraying new roles for women in the world of work and new roles for both sexes in the home.

The counselor's office is not immune to myths about women's place, capabilities, natural preferences, and suitabilities. Counselors should help both sexes distinguish between biological realities and cultural inventions. Sex role standards are a prime example of a pervasive cultural invention. Although these standards are in a state of flux and it appears that psychological androgyny is on the horizon, it is the youth of each generation that determines the cultural inventions of the coming decades—as Margaret Mead reminds us in *Culture and Commitment.*[6] Counselors can work with other school staff in helping youth understand the limitations of traditional sex role standards in the context of our current technology, our family and social institutions, and our increasingly female work force. Counselors can also help youth identify ways in which myths about women have served to socialize both sexes to accept a sex stereotyped world, a world that is rapidly becoming outmoded by recent state and federal legislative actions, executive orders, and court rulings.

The Women's Bureau of the U.S. Department of Labor widely distributed a list of myths and realities about women that can be helpful in combating the myth that the prospect of marriage and a career creates an either/or situation for women. For example, the Women's Bureau reports that nine out of ten women will work at some time in their lives, most of them because of pressing economic need. Furthermore, fewer and fewer women leave work for marriage and children. Of those who do take a break to have children,

63

most return to work when their children are in school. Even with a break in employment the average woman worker may expect to work for 25 years, and many work up to 45 years.

Myths about certain careers being more compatible with women's roles have been perpetuated by means of biased textbooks, sexist careers materials, and even well-meaning counselors. Women have been depicted in extremely limited roles in school textbooks in all subject areas. For example, a detailed analysis of 2,760 short stories from elementary school reading texts found that men were shown in 147 different occupations, but women were shown in only 25.[7] Some of the 25 female occupations were of dubious economic value (e.g., witch, queen, fat lady in a circus).

In a comprehensive study of post–1970 high school level career guidance materials, Vetter and others found sex role stereotyping in almost all of the 9,500 pages and 1,850 illustrations analyzed.[8] Since differences in achievement appear to be heavily dependent upon student perception of given areas (e.g., mathematics, reading, science) as sex appropriate or sex inappropriate, the subtle messages about careers found in most materials have strong implications for the counselor intent on combating myths.[9,10,11]

However, before counselors can combat the myths afloat in the media and elsewhere, they need to get the cobwebs out of their own corners. In a review of research on counselor sex bias, Schlossberg and Pietofesa found definite indications that counselors ascribe particular sex roles to men and women and that counselor interview behavior reflects these biases.[12] Nor is this bias limited to male counselors. Thomas and Stewart, for example, found that both male and female counselors rated female clients with "deviate" (i.e., not traditionally female) career goals to be more in need of counseling than those with "conforming" (i.e., traditionally feminine) goals.[13] Ahrons found that counselors perceive women's career roles to be isolated from or incompatible with other female roles.[14]

Counselors need to examine their belief systems about women based upon facts, preferred futures, and current projections. Is it true, as Broverman and associates suggest, that counselors of both sexes see healthy women as differing from healthy men by being less objective, less independent, less adventurous, less aggressive, less competitive, more submissive, more easily influenced, more emotional, more excitable in minor crises, more likely to have their feelings hurt, more conceited about their appearance, and as having a dislike for math and science?[15] If so, is it not likely that these expectations and other myths will become self-fulfilling prophecies?

There are at least two reasons why counselors should become closer to the instructional process. Studies have shown that student-expressed need for help in career planning is in sharp contrast to the help students feel they have received from their counselors.[16] Preliminary findings of the National Longitudinal Study of the High School Class of 1972 indicate the typical counselor has an average case load of about 350 students and spends less than one-fourth of his or her time working with students on career or educational concerns.[17]

Some counselors are attempting to extend their contacts by using group counseling. Teachers and administrators should invite counselors to participate in instruction. Counselors often have skills in assertive behavior training, values clarification, the psychology of women, and small group discussion that may prove valuable in survival lessons for women.

Direct Teaching/Counseling

- Conduct career workshops in nontraditional careers for both sexes.

- Establish a resource file for students and teachers.

- Counsel girls to move toward freedom from sex role stereotypes.

- Counter myths with facts about women's place and potential.

- Train teaching teams to conduct assertive behavior training, to conduct values clarification exercises, and to discuss feminism.

Indirect Teaching/Counseling

- Select nonsexist career guidance materials.

- Become aware of ways to avoid counselor bias.

17. Extracurriculum and Administration

Because the extracurriculum of the school is important to students; it is subject to the same guidelines on sex role stereotyping as the curriculum. Students learn about the importance of women's roles from the trophy cases in the hall and from staffing patterns in the principal's office.

School sponsored events and trips should be equally accessible to girls and boys. Service and hobby clubs should encourage equal participation by both sexes. For example, the audio-visual equipment of the school is often maintained by capable students who learn about the technical operation and care of equipment. But if only boys are expected to know about such things, students learn to associate such tasks with males.

There is some evidence from counseling research that engineers may be more likely to have had various model-building hobbies. Gordon Odegaard found in his Piagetian research that young boys perform linear spatial arrangement tasks with miniature telephone poles more easily than young girls.[1] He noted how frequently the boys referred to previously play with model trains and how familiar the tasks appeared to them. Girls need early experiences with model building and electric trains, too.

Bands and orchestras often display sex role stereotyping in the frequency with which boys and girls play certain instruments. In some districts both boys and girls enjoy the violin through upper elementary. But at that point, a negative image sometimes appears to drive the boys away from this instrument—perhaps to the greater masculine safety of the trumpet, the tuba, and the bass and kettle drums.

In recent years, cheerleaders have usually been girls. Boys may try out for the squad, but they often suffer, as the central character in C. H. Frick's teen-age novel, *Comeback Guy*, discovered.[2] Awkward attempts have been made to preserve male representation on squads by reviving the term "yell leader." Girls, however, continue to be called cheerleaders. Meanwhile, other supportive roles in athletic pageants such as pom-pom girl and baton twirler are even more heavily occupied by females.

Junior versions of community service clubs represent another category of extracurricular activity. Teen-age clubs, such as the satellites of Kiwanis, have reportedly voted to become coeducational, but their elders managed to get a specific exemption to Title IX regulations for just such clubs. Unless administrators, teachers, students, and school board members decide that both sexes have a right to membership and that this right is based upon a higher level of ethics than that represented by the Title IX regulations, these clubs will no doubt continue to function on the school premises in a sex segregated fashion.

Young women need to see successful female managerial role models in their everyday lives. Women executives should not be so rare that they appear only in human interest stories in obscure journals. If we believe we live in a pluralistic society, we should expect to see and encourage the development of leaders from all segments of our society. Administrators are familiar with the staffing philosophy that calls for a balanced representation among the teachers. Some superintendents have extended this philosophy to their administrative teams, but this ideal has seldom included women. A balance of males and females on a school system's administrative team is likely to create more balanced planning and management of the extracurriculum—which depends heavily on administrative guidance.

Direct Steps Toward Remediation

- Encourage club sponsors, officers, and others to recruit equitable numbers of both sexes.

- If some extracurricular organizations persist in sexual discrimination in the face of repeated efforts to reform them, deny them the use of school premises for their activities.

- Refuse to accept awards from organizations outside the school that practice sexual and racial discrimination.

- Hire and support women administrators. A survey of a medium-sized school system will usually disclose several women faculty who have administrative credentials. In addition, colleges of education are graduating increasing numbers of women with advanced degrees in educational administration. These graduates are often more mobile than their predecessors.

- Design intern programs within your school district. Have a combination of types: some may be for a full year, others for a few months on a rotating basis.

- Sponsor women who show interest and ability in administration. Encourage them to oversee activities in the school district that gave them managerial knowledge. Ask them to join committees that have significant responsibilities, such as the negotiations team.

Indirect Teaching

- Sponsors of model building, chess, math games, science, and related clubs should work with counselors to encourage more girls to join and enjoy such groups.

- Music teachers should encourage members of both sexes to avoid sex stereotyped choices when selecting musical instruments.

- Conduct an overall evaluation of the extracurricular program in connection with a school accreditation visit. Pay particular attention to problems of sex discrimination.

- Give women visible leadership roles, such as assuming reponsibility for assembly programs and public relations.

- Encourage women to attend administrative conferences and meetings on women's studies and Title IX.

- Take women to meetings where they can listen to the shoptalk of other administrators and see how problems are ironed out.

- Encourage women to develop sports coaching and officiating knowledge.

References and Bibliography

References

Chapter One—Introduction: Women's Studies K-12

1. Gunnar Myrdal, *An American Dilemma: The Negro Problem and Modern Democracy* (New York: Harper and Brothers, 1944).

Chapter Two—Need for Changes in Sex Roles

1. Patrick C. Lee and Nancy B. Gropper, "A Cultural Analysis of Sex Role in the Schools," *Journal of Teacher Education* 26, no. 4 (Winter 1975): 335–39.
2. *Ibid.*
3. Jessie Bernard, *The Future of Marriage* (New York: World Publishing Co., 1972).
4. *Title IX of the Education Amendments of 1972*, 20 U.S.C. §1681 et seq.
5. U.S. Department of Health, Education and Welfare, Office for Civil Rights, *Final Title IX Regulation Implementing Education Amendments of 1972 Prohibiting Sex Discrimination in Education* (Washington, D.C.: U.S. Department of Health, Education and Welfare, June 1975).
6. U.S. Department of Health, Education and Welfare, Office of Education, "Women's Educational Equity Act Program," *Federal Register* 41, no. 30, 12 February 1971.
7. Institute for Educational Leadership, *Handbook on How to End Sexism in Your Schools*, IEL Reports: Five (Washington, D.C.: George Washington University, August 1975).
8. *Decade for Women: World Plan of Action* (Washington, D.C.: Women's Equity Action League, undated).

Chapter Three—Women's Studies on the College Campus

1. Florence Howe and Carol Ahlum, "Women's Studies and Social Change," in *Academic Women on the Move*, eds. Alice S. Rossi and Ann Caldewood (New York: Russell Sage Foundation, 1973), pp. 393–423.
2. Deborah Rosenfelt, *Female Studies VII: Going Strong—New Courses/New Programs* (Old Westbury, N.Y.: Feminist Press, 1973), p. iii.
3. Shirley McCune and Martha Matthews, "Women's Studies and Teacher Education: Actuality and Potential," *Journal of Teacher Education* 26, no. 4 (Winter 1975): 340–44.
4. *Ibid.*
5. *Ibid.*

Chapter Four—Definitions, Concepts, and Theories

1. U.S. Department of Health, Education and Welfare, Office of Education, "Women's Educational Equity Act Program," *Federal Register* 41, no. 30, 12 February 1971.

2. J. Kagan, "Acquisition and Significance of Sex Typing and Sex Role Identity," in *Review of Child Development Research,* vol. I, ed. M. L. Hoffman (New York: Russell Sage Foundation, 1964), pp. 137–67.
3. Eleanor Maccoby and Carol Nagy Jacklin, "What We Know and Don't Know About Sex Differences," *Psychology Today,* December 1974, pp. 109–12.
4. Debra Waber, "Sex Differences in Cognition: A Function of Maturation Rate?" *Science* 192, no. 4239 (5 May 1976): 572–3.
5. J. B. Stroud and E. F. Lindquist, "Sex Differences in Achievement in the Elementary and Secondary Schools," *Journal of Educational Psychology* 33 (1942): 659.
6. Muriel James and Dorothy Jongward, *Born To Win: Transactional Analysis with Gestalt Experiments* (Reading, Mass.: Addison-Wesley Publishing Co., 1973), p. 69.
7. Claude Steiner, *Scripts People Live: Transactional Analysis of Life Scripts* (New York: Grove Press, Inc., 1974).
8. H. Bandura, "Social Learning Theory of Identificatory Processes," in *Handbook on Socialization Theory and Research,* ed. David A. Gaslin (Chicago: Rand McNally and Co., 1969), p. 215.
9. Lawrence Kohlberg, "A Cognitive Development Analysis of Children's Sex Role Concepts and Attitudes," in *The Development of Sex Difference,* ed. E. E. Maccoby (Stanford, Cal.: Stanford University Press, 1966).
10. Eleanor Maccoby and Carol Nagy Jacklin, *The Psychology of Sex Differences* (Stanford, Cal.: Stanford University Press, 1974), p. 364.
11. *Ibid.*
12. J. Kagan 1964.
13. L. Festinger, *A Theory of Cognitive Dissonance* (Evanston, Ill.: Row, Peterson, 1957).

Chapter Five—A New Model: Psychological Androgyny

1. J. Kagan, "Acquisition and Significance of Sex Typing and Sex Role Identity," in *Review of Child Development Research,* vol. I, ed. M. L. Hoffman (New York: Russell Sage Foundation, 1964), pp. 137–67.
2. Sandra Bem, "Sex Role Adaptability: One Consequence of Psychological Androgyny," *Journal of Personality and Social Psychology* 31, no. 4 (1975): 634–43.
3. A. L. Edwards, *The Social Desirability Variable in Personality Assessment and Research* (New York: Dryden, 1957).
4. I. K. Broverman et al., "Sex Role Stereotypes: A Current Appraisal," *Journal of Social Issues* 28, no. 2 (1972): 59–78.
5. P. Rosenkrantz et al., "Sex Role Stereotypes and Self-Concepts in College Students," *Journal of Counseling and Clinical Psychology* 32, no. 3 (1968): 287–95.
6. I. K. Broverman et al., "Sex and Role Stereotypes and Clinical Judgments of Mental Health," *Journal of Consulting Psychology* 34 (1970): 1–7.
7. Simone de Beauvior, *The Second Sex* (New York: Bantam Books, 1961).

8. Patricia Jakubowski-Spector, "Facilitating the Growth of Women Through Assertive Training," *The Counseling Psychologist* 4, no. 1 (1973): 75–86.
9. Lynn Z. Bloom, Karen Coburn, and Joan Pearlman, *The New Assertive Woman* (New York: Delacorte Press, 1975).
10. Patrick C. Lee and Nancy B. Gropper, "A Cultural Analysis of Sex Role in the Schools," *Journal of Teacher Education* 26, no. 4 (Winter 1975): 335–39.
11. Margaret Mead, *Culture and Commitment: A Study of the Generation Gap* (Garden City, N.Y.: Natural History Press—Doubleday, 1970).
12. Louis E. Raths, Merrill Harmin, and Sidney B. Simon, *Values and Teaching: Working with Values in the Classroom* (Columbus, Ohio: Charles E. Merrill, 1966).

Chapter Six—Implementation

1. Resource Center on Sex Roles, *Today's Changing Roles: An Approach to Nonsexist Teaching* (Washington, D.C.: National Foundation for the Improvement of Education, 1974).

Chapter Seven—Reading and Language Arts

1. Women on Words and Images, *Dick and Jane As Victims: Sex Stereotyping in Children's Readers* (Princeton, N.J.: Women on Words and Images, 1972).
2. Leslie Z. McArthur and Susan V. Eisen, "Achievements of Male and Female Storybook Characters As Determinants of Achievement Behavior by Boys and Girls," *Journal of Personality and Social Psychology* 33, no. 4 (1976): 467–73.
3. Margaret B. McDowell, "Beyond Women's Studies?" *Iowa English Bulletin Yearbook* 24, no. 3 (1974): 41–48.

Chapter Eight—Social Studies

1. Janice Law Trecker, "Women in U.S. History High School Textbooks," *Social Education* 35, no. 3 (March 1971): 249.
2. William H. Chafe, *The American Woman: Her Changing Social, Economic, and Political Roles 1920–1970* (London: Oxford University Press, 1972).
3. Betty Friedan, *The Feminine Mystique* (New York: W. W. Norton and Co., 1963).
4. *Herstory* (Lakeside, Cal.: Interact Co., undated).

Chapter Nine—Mathematics

1. Eleanor Maccoby and Carol Nagy Jacklin, *The Psychology of Sex Differences* (Stanford, Cal.: Stanford University Press, 1974).
2. Eleanor Maccoby, "Sex Differences in Intellectual Functioning," in *The Development of Sex Differences*, ed. E. E. Maccoby (Stanford, Cal.: Stanford University Press, 1966).

3. Eleanor Maccoby and Carol Nagy Jacklin, "What We Know and Don't Know About Sex Differences," *Psychology Today*, December 1974, p. 111.
4. Maccoby, "Sex Differences in Intellectual Functioning," 1966.
5. Lenore J. Weitzman and Diane Rizzo, *Biased Textbooks* (Washington, D.C.: Resource Center on Sex Roles in Education, 1974).
6. Cited in J. Ernest, *Mathematics and Sex* (Santa Barbara, Cal.: Mathematics Department, University of California at Santa Barbara, 1976), p. 6.
7. Cited in J. Ernest, pp. 2–10.
8. Carnegie Commission on Higher Education, *Priorities for Action: Final Report of the Carnegie Commission on Higher Education* (New York: McGraw Hill Book Co., 1975).
9. H. Luchins, *Women in Mathematics: Problems of Orientation and Reorientation* (Troy, N.Y.: Rensslaer Polytechnic Institute, 1975).
10. Sheila Tobias, "Math Anxiety: Why Is a Smart Girl Like You Counting on Your Fingers?" *Ms.* 5, no. 3 (September 1976): 56.

Chapter Ten—Science

1. B. W. Vetter and E. L. Babco, *Professional Women and Minorities* (Washington, D.C.: Scientific Manpower Commission, 1975).
2. Lenore J. Weitzman and Diane Rizzo, *Biased Textbooks* (Washington, D.C.: Resource Center on Sex Roles in Education, 1974).
3. Dale J. Prediger, Gail T. McLure, and Richard J. Noeth, *Promoting the Exploration of Personally Relevant Career Options in Science and Technology* (Iowa City, Iowa: American College Testing Program, 1976).
4. Gail T. McLure, *Women in Science and Technology* (Iowa City, Iowa: American College Testing Program, 1976).
5. U.S. Department of Labor, Bureau of Labor Statistics, "Looking Ahead to a Career—A Slide Show" (Washington, D.C., 1975).

Chapter Eleven

1. Conversation with Gladys Scott, Professor Emeritus, Physical Education, University of Iowa, Iowa City, fall, 1976.

Chapter Twelve—Fine Arts

1. Sophie Drinker, *Music and Women* (New York: Coward-McCann, Inc., 1948).

Chapter Thirteen—Home Economics

1. Betty Roszak and Theodore Roszak, eds., *Masculine/Feminine: Readings in Sexual Mythology and the Liberation of Women* (New York: Harper and Row, 1969).
2. Jessie Bernard, *The Future of Marriage* (New York: World Publishing Co., 1972).
3. American College Testing Program, *Perspectives of a Changing*

World: A Survey of Ohio High School Students 1975–1976 (Iowa City, Iowa: American College Testing Program, 1977).

4. Elizabeth Simpson, "Women's Lib Is Here To Stay: A Clarion Call to Vocational Education," *American Vocational Journal* 45, no. 9 (December 1970): 18.

Chapter Fourteen—Foreign Language

1. Motoko Y. Lee, "The Married Woman's Status and Role as Reflected in Japanese: An Exploratory Sociolinguistic Study," *Signs, Journal of Women in Culture and Society* 1 (Summer 1976): 993.

Chapter Fifteen—Industrial Arts and Vocational Education

1. American Vocational Association Revision Committee, *A Guide to Improving Instruction in Industrial Arts* (Washington, D.C.: American Vocational Association, 1968).
2. "The Seven Cardinal Principles Revisited," *Today's Education* 65, no. 3 (September-October 1976): 65.

Chapter Sixteen—Counseling

1. Martha Matthews and Shirley McCune, *Complying with Title IX: Implementing Institutional Self-Evaluation* (Washington, D.C.: Resource Center on Sex Roles in Education, National Foundation for the Improvement of Education, 1976).
2. Barbara Cook and Beverly Stone, *Counseling Women,* (Boston: Houghton Mifflin Co., 1973).
3. M. E. Verheyden-Hilliard, *Resources for Counselors, Teachers, and Administrators,* rev. ed. (Washington, D.C.: American Personnel and Guidance Association, undated).
4. *Sex Fairness in Career Guidance: A Learning Kit* (Cambridge, Mass.: ABT Publications, 1975).
5. E. Matthews and D. V. Tiedeman, "Attitudes Toward Career and Marriage and the Development of Life Styles in Young Women," *Journal of Counseling Psychology* 2 (1964): 375–84.
6. Margaret Mead, *Culture and Commitment: A Study of the Generation Gap* (Garden City, N.Y.: Natural History Press—Doubleday, 1970).
7. Women on Words and Images, *Dick and Jane As Victims: Sex Stereotyping in Children's Readers* (Princeton, N.J.: Women on Words and Images, 1972).
8. L. Vetter, D. W. Stockburger, and C. Brose, *Career Guidance Materials: Implications for Women's Career Developments* (Columbus, Ohio: Center for Vocational Education, Ohio State University, 1974).
9. C. A. Dwyer, "Influences of Children's Sex Role Standards on Reading and Arithmetic Achievement," *Journal of Educational Psychology* 66 (1974): 811–16.
10. J. Kagan, "Acquisition and Significance of Sex Typing and Sex Role Identity," in *Review of Child Development Research*, vol. I, ed. M. L. Hoffman (New York: Russell Sage Foundation, 1964), pp. 137–67.

11. P. S. Houts and D. R. Entwisle, "Academic Achievement Effort Among Females: Achievement Attitudes and Sex-Role Orientation," *Journal of Counseling Psychology* 15 (1968): 284–6.
12. N. K. Schlossberg and J. J. Pietofesa, "Perspectives on Counseling Bias: Implications for Counseling Education," *Counseling Psychology* 4 (1973): 44–54.
13. A. H. Thomas and N. R. Stewart, "Counselor Response to Female Clients with Deviate and Conforming Goals," *Journal of Counseling Psychology* 18 (1971): 352–57.
14. C. R. Ahrons, "Counselor's Perceptions of Career Images of Women," *Journal of Vocational Behavior* 8 (1976): 197–207.
15. I. K. Broverman et al., (1970).
16. D. J. Prediger, J. D. Roth, and R. J. Noeth, *Nationwide Study of Student Career Development: Summary of Results* (Iowa City, Iowa: American College Testing Program, 1973).
17. "How Counselor's Time Is Spent," *Guidepost* 16, no. 7 (1973): 2.

Chapter Seventeen—Extracurriculum and Administration

1. Gordon Odegaard, "An Investigation of Piaget's Groupings: Seriation and Projective Space," Ph.D. dissertation, University of Iowa, 1975.
2. C. H. Frick, *Comeback Guy* (New York: Harcourt, 1961).

Bibliography

Ahrons, C. R. "Counselor's Perceptions of Career Images of Women." *Journal of Vocational Behavior* 8 (1976): 197–207.

American College Testing Program. *Perspectives of a Changing World: A Survey of Ohio High School Students 1975–1976.* Iowa City, Iowa: American College Testing Program, 1977.

American Vocational Association Revision Committee. *A Guide to Improving Instruction in Industrial Arts.* Washington, D.C.: American Vocational Association, 1968.

Bandura, H. "Social Learning Theory of Identificatory Processes." In *Handbook of Socialization Theory and Research,* edited by David A. Gaslin. Chicago: Rand McNally and Company, 1969.

Bem, Sandra. "Sex Role Adaptibility: One Consequence of Psychological Androgyny." *Journal of Personality and Social Psychology* 31, no. 4 (1975): 634–43.

Bernard, Jessie. *The Future of Marriage.* New York: World Publishing Co., 1972.

Bloom, Lynn Z.; Coburn, Karen; and Pearlman, Joan. *The New Assertive Woman.* New York: Delacorte Press, 1975.

Broverman, I. K.; Vogel, S. R.; Broverman, D. M.; Clarkson, F. E.; and Rosenkrantz, P. S. "Sex Role Stereotypes: A Current Appraisal." *Journal of Social Issues* 28, no. 2 (1972): 59–78.

Broverman, I. K.; Broverman, D. M.; Clarkson, F. E.; Rosenkrantz, P.; and Vogel, S. R. "Sex and Role Stereotypes and Clinical Judgments of Mental Health." *Journal of Consulting Psychology* 34 (1970): 1–7.

Carnegie Commission on Higher Education. *Priorities for Action: Final Report of The Carnegie Commission on Higher Education with Technical Notes and Appendices.* New York: McGraw Hill Book Co., 1975.

Chafe, William H. *The American Woman: Her Changing Social, Economic, and Political Roles 1920–1970.* London: Oxford University Press, 1972.

Cook, Barbara, and Stone, Beverly, *Counseling Women* (Boston: Houghton Mifflin Co., 1973).

De Beauvoir, Simone. *The Second Sex.* New York: Bantam Books, 1961.

Decade for Women: World Plan of Action. Washington, D.C.: Women's Equity Action League Educational and Legal Defense Fund, undated.

Drinker, Sophie. *Music and Women.* New York: Coward-McCann, Inc., 1948.

Dwyer, C. A. "Influences of Children's Sex Role Standards on Reading and Arithmetic Achievement." *Journal of Educational Psychology* 66 (1974): 811–816.

Edwards, A. L. *The Social Desirability Variable in Personality Assessment and Research.* New York: Dryden, 1957.

Ernest, J. *Mathematics and Sex.* Santa Barbara, Cal.: Mathematics Department, University of California at Santa Barbara, 1975.

Farrell, Warren. *The Liberated Man.* New York: Random House, 1975.

Festinger, L. *A Theory of Cognitive Dissonance*. Evanston, Ill.: Row, Peterson, 1957.

Frick, C. H. *Comeback Guy*. New York: Harcourt, 1961.

Friedan, Betty. *The Feminine Mystique*. New York: W. W. Norton and Co., 1963.

Herstory. Lakeside, Cal. Interact Co., undated.

Houts, P. S., and Entwisle, D. R. "Academic Achievement Effort Among Females: Achievement Attitudes and Sex-Role Orientation," *Journal of Counseling Psychology* 15 (1968): 284–6.

"How Counselor's Time Is Spent." *Guidepost* 16, no. 7 (1973): 2.

Howe, Florence, and Ahlum, Carol. "Women's Studies and Social Change." In *Academic Women on the Move*, edited by Alice S. Rossi and Ann Caldewood, pp. 393–423. New York: Russell Sage Foundation, 1973.

Institute for Educational Leadership. *Handbook on How To End Sexism in Your Schools*, a position paper prepared by the National Conference on Women in Educational Policy Making (IEL Reports: Five). Washington, D.C.: George Washington University, August 1975.

Jakubowski-Spector, Patricia. "Facilitating the Growth of Women Through Assertive Training," *The Counseling Psychologist* 4, no. 1 (1973): 75–86.

James, Muriel, and Jongeward, Dorothy. *Born To Win: Transactional Analysis with Gestalt Experiments*. Reading, Mass.: Addison-Wesley Publishing Company, 1973.

Kagan, J. "Acquisition and Significance of Sex Typing and Sex Role Identity." In *Review of Child Development Research*, Vol. I, edited by M. L. Hoffman, pp. 137–67. New York: Russell Sage Foundation, 1964.

Kohlberg, Lawrence. "A Cognitive Development Analysis of Children's Sex Roles Concepts and Attitudes." In *The Development of Sex Difference*, edited by E. E. Maccoby. Stanford, Cal.: Stanford University Press, 1966.

Lee, Motoko Y., "The Married Woman's Status and Role as Reflected in Japanese: An Exploratory Sociolinguistic Study," *Signs, Journal of Women in Culture and Society* 1, no. 4 (Summer 1976): 991–99.

Lee, Patrick C., and Gropper, Nancy B. "A Cultural Analysis of Sex Role in the Schools." *Journal of Teacher Education* 26, no. 4 (Winter 1975): 335–39.

Luchins, H. *Women in Mathematics: Problems of Orientation and Reorientation* (Final Report: National Science Foundation Grant GY-11316). Troy, N. Y.: Renssalaer Polytechnic Institute, 1975.

Maccoby, Eleanor. "Sex Differences in Intellectual Functioning." In *The Development of Sex Differences*, edited by E. E. Maccoby. Stanford, Cal.: Stanford University Press, 1966.

Maccoby, Eleanor, and Jacklin, Carol Nagy. *The Psychology of Sex Differences*. Stanford, Cal.: Stanford University Press, 1974.

——————. "What We Know and Don't Know About Sex Differences." *Psychology Today*. December 1974, pp. 109–12.

Matthews, Martha, and McCune, Shirley. *Complying with Title IX: Implementing Institutional Self-Evaluation*. Washington, D.C.: Resource Center on Sex Roles in Education, National Foundation for the Improvement of Education, 1976.

Matthews, E., and Tiedeman, D. V. "Attitudes Toward Career and Marriage and the Development of Life Styles in Young Women." *Journal of Counseling Psychology* 2 (1964): 375–84.

McArthur, Leslie Z., and Eisen, Susan V. "Achievements of Male and Female Storybook Characters As Determinants of Achievement Behavior by Boys and Girls." *Journal of Personality and Social Psychology* 33, no. 4 (1976): 467–73.

McCune, Shirley, and Matthews, Martha. "Women's Studies and Teacher Education: Actuality and Potential." *Journal of Teacher Education* 26, no. 4 (Winter 1975): 340–44.

McLure, Gail T. *Women in Science and Technology.* Iowa City, Iowa: American College Testing Program, 1976.

McDowell, Margaret B. "Beyond Women's Studies?" *Iowa English Bulletin Yearbook* 24, no. 3 (1974): 41–48.

Mead, Margaret. *Culture and Commitment: A Study of the Generation Gap.* Garden City, N.Y.: Natural History Press—Doubleday & Co., Inc., 1970.

Myrdal, Gunnar. *An American Dilemma: The Negro Problem and Modern Democracy.* New York: Harper and Brothers, 1944.

Odegaard, Gordon. "An Investigation of Piaget's Groupings: Seriation and Projective Space." Ph.D. dissertation, University of Iowa, 1975.

The Patron: The Official Song Book of the Grange. Rev. ed. Washington, D.C., 1954.

Prediger, D. J.; Roth, J. D.; and Noeth, R. J. *Nationwide Study of Student Career Development: Summary of Results* (ACT Research Report No. 61). Iowa City, Iowa: American College Testing Program, 1973.

Prediger, Dale J., McLure, Gail T., and Richard J. Noeth. *Promoting the Exploration of Personally Relevant Career Options in Science and Technology* (Final Report: National Science Foundation Grant No. SM175-18149). Iowa City, Iowa: American College Testing Program, 1976.

Raths, Louis E.; Harmin, Merrill; and Simon, Sidney B. *Values and Teaching: Working with Values in the Classroom.* Columbus, Ohio: Charles E. Merrill, 1966.

Resource Center on Sex Roles. *Today's Changing Roles: An Approach to Nonsexist Teaching.* Washington, D.C.: National Foundation for the Improvement of Education, 1974.

Rosenfelt, Deborah. *Female Studies VII: Going Strong—New Courses/New Programs.* Old Westbury, N.Y.: Feminist Press, 1973.

Rosenkrantz, P.; Vogel, S. R.; Bee, H.; Broverman, I. K.; and Broverman, D. M. "Sex Role Stereotypes and Self-Concepts in College Students." *Journal of Counseling and Clinical Psychology* 32, no. 3 (1968): 287–95.

Roszak, Betty, and Roszak, Theodore eds. *Masculine/Feminine: Readings in Sexual Mythology and the Liberation of Women.* New York: Harper and Row, 1969.

Schlossberg, N. K., and Pietofesa, J. J. "Perspectives on Counseling Bias: Implications for Counseling Education." *Counseling Psychology* 4 (1973): 44–54.

Sex Fairness in Career Guidance: A Learning Kit. Cambridge, Mass.: ABT Publications, 1975.

79

Simpson, Elizabeth. "Women's Lib Is Here To Stay: A Clarion Call to Vocational Education" *American Vocational Journal* 45, no. 9 (December 1970): 18.

Steiner, Claude. *Scripts People Live: Transactional Analysis of Life Scripts.* New York: Grove Press, Inc., 1974.

Stroud, J. B., and Lindquist, E. F. "Sex Differences in Achievement in the Elementary and Secondary Schools." *Journal of Educational Psychology* 33 (1942): 659.

Thomas, A. H., and Stewart, N. R. "Counselor Response to Female Clients with Deviate and Conforming Goals." *Journal of Counseling Psychology* 18 (1971): 352–57.

Title IX of the Education Amendments of 1972. 20 U.S.C. § 1681 et seq.

Tobias, Sheila. "Math Anxiety: Why is a Smart Girl Like You Counting on Your Fingers?" *Ms.* 5, no. 3 (September 1976): 56.

"The Seven Cardinal Principles Revisited." *Today's Education* 65, no. 3 (September-October 1976): 65.

Trecker, Janice Law. "Women in U.S. History High School Textbooks." *Social Education* 35, no. 3 (March 1971): 249.

U.S. Department of Health, Education and Welfare, Office for Civil Rights. *Final Title IX Regulation Implementing Education Amendments of 1972 Prohibiting Sex Discrimination in Education.* Washington, D.C.: U.S. Department of Health, Education and Welfare, June 1975.

U.S. Department of Health, Education and Welfare, Office of Education. "Women's Educational Equity Act Program." *Federal Register* 41, no. 30; 12 February 1976.

U.S. Department of Labor, Bureau of Labor Statistics. "Looking Ahead to a Career—A Slide Show." Washington, D.C., 1975.

Verheyden-Hilliard, M. E. *Resources for Counselors, Teachers, and Administrators.* Rev. ed. Washington, D.C.: Opportunities Project, American Personnel and Guidance Association, undated.

Vetter, B. W., and Babco, E. L. *Professional Women and Minorities.* Washington, D.C.: Scientific Manpower Commission, 1975.

Vetter, L.; Stockburger, D. W.; and Brose, C. *Career Guidance Materials: Implications for Women's Career Development.* Columbus, Ohio: Center for Vocational Education, Ohio State University, 1974.

Waber, Debra. "Sex Differences in Cognition: A Function of Maturation Rate?" *Science* 192, no. 4239 (May 5, 1976): pp. 572–3.

Weitzman, Lenore J., and Rizzo, Diane. *Biased Textbooks.* Washington, D.C.: Resource Center on Sex Roles in Education, 1974.

Women on Words and Images. *Dick and Jane As Victims: Sex Stereotyping in Children's Readers.* Princeton, N.J.: Women on Words and Images, 1972.